Akane
Immigrant Poet

The Tanka of Mitsuko Kasuga,
a Japanese Immigrant in Mexico

移民歌人
あかね

在メキシコ日系移民・春日光子とその短歌 ［英語版］

INDEX
目次

PROLOGUE 6
はじめに

MESSAGE FOR THE ENGLISH EDITION 9
刊行によせて

Part I
100 SELECTED TANKA
第一部　短歌百選

LEGEND 14
凡例

I. CROSSING THE OCEAN 15
I. 海をわたる

II. MY CHILDREN 18
II. 子への思い

III. MY HUSBAND 45
III. 夫への思い

IV. ADAPTED SPIRIT,
PERSISTENT VALUES 49
  IV. 揺れる心、変わらぬ信念

V. DAILY LIFE 63
  V. 暮らしの中で

VI. MY LAND 73
  VI. ふるさと

VII. MY GRANDCHILDREN 86
  VII. 孫への思い

VIII. WITHOUT YOU 99
  VIII. 夫 逝く

BIOGRAPHY I 124
  略歴 I

Part II
THE LIFE OF MITSUKO KASUGA

第二部　春日光子の生涯

MAP 128
地図

1. A JAPANESE GIRL WITH AN AMBITIOUS SPIRIT 130
1. 信州育ちの勝ち気な娘

2. BECOMING A "PICTURE BRIDE" 136
2.「写真花嫁」

3. A NEW HOME IN MEXICO 145
3. 新天地メキシコ

4. LIFE IN CERRITOS 150
4. セリートスでの慣れない暮らし

5. OPENING A STORE ON THE EVE OF WAR 155
5. 戦争前夜の店開き

6. FORCED MIGRATION 161
6. 強制移住

7. STARTING OVER AFTER THE WAR 167
7. 戦後の新規まき直し

8. RAISING SIX CHILDREN 174
8. 六人の子育て

9. A TIME FOR EDUCATION 178
9. 暮らしの安定と教育への熱意

10. TANKA AND THE CACTUS 187
　10. 短歌とサボテン

11. A FAMILY REUNION 192
　11. 父との再会

12. FULL-SCALE BUSINESS EXPANSION 196
　12. 事業の拡大

13. AN EXTENDED FAMILY 200
　13. 大所帯

14. PAST AND FUTURE MEET IN JAPAN 204
　14. 日本とのつながり

15. GRANDCHILDREN ARRIVE 209
　15. 孫の誕生

16. MEXICAN PRIDE 216
　16. メキシコの誇り

17. DEATH COMES SUDDENLY 221
　17. 夫の急逝

18. CREATIVE MATURITY 228
　18. 歌人としての成熟

19. QUIET LATER YEARS 236
　19. 穏やかな晩年

BIOGRAPHY II 244
　略歴 II

PROLOGUE
はじめに

Aiko Chikaba
近葉 愛子

Tanka is a distinctly Japanese form of poetry that dates back over 1,300 years. Tanka poems consist of fixed verses of 31 characters and have a unique syllabic rhythm of 5-7-5-7-7. It is used to express emotions and inspiration found in everyday life, covering topics from familial love and romantic feelings to aspects of everyday life. In contrast to haiku, which is well known for being the world's shortest fixed verse, tanka uses more syllables, and does not require the use of a seasonal term. For these reasons, one could argue that tanka allows greater freedom of expression than haiku.

This project began a number of years ago when my husband, a third-generation Japanese, casually handed me a collection of poems. He said they

短歌は日本文化を代表する三十一文字の定型詩で、実に1300年もの歴史があります。自然や生活の中で心動かされたことを「五‐七‐五‐七‐七」のリズムにのせて表現するのが特徴です。「世界一短い定型詩」として知られる俳句と比べ、短歌は文字数が多く、季語を入れるという決まりもありません。そのため家族への愛情や恋、日常生活の中で感じたことなど、さまざまな題材について自由に歌うことができる形式だと言えます。

私が歌集『短歌 あかね』に出会ったのは数年前のこと。日系三世である私の夫・カルロスが、僕のおばあちゃんが遺した本だといって何気なく手渡してくれたのが始まりでした。ページをめくるとすぐ、素直で力強い短歌のリズムを通して伝わってくる光子おばあちゃんの生き様に、私はぐいぐい引き込まれていきました。

信州に生まれ育った春日光子（雅号・あかね/1914～2002年）がまだ見ぬ日本

はじめに　PROLOGUE

had been written by his deceased grandmother, but that he'd never read them because they were written in classic Japanese. As I turned the pages, I was drawn more and more into Grandma Mitsuko's tanka, which had an honest strength to its rhythm and provided insights into her life.

Born in Japan, Mitsuko Kasuga (1914-2002) traveled to Mexico in 1936 to marry a Japanese immigrant she'd never met. She was 22 years old at the time.

Throughout her adult life in Mexico, writing tanka gave her the strength to face life, whether she was filled with joy, consumed by anger, or gripped by heart-wrenching sadness. It wasn't until she turned 70 years old that Mitsuko published a collection of her tanka under the pen name *Akane*. It was titled

人移民のもとに嫁ぐため、海を越えてメキシコに渡ったのは22歳のときでした。新天地メキシコでの厳しい暮らしの中で、光子の心を支えたものが短歌だったといえるでしょう。楽しいときも、怒りがこみあげてくるときも、悲しみで胸が張り裂けそうなときも、歌を詠むことが生きる力となっていたのです。その集大成として光子は、70歳を迎えた年に歌集『短歌 あかね』を出版しました。

本書の「第一部 短歌百選」では、『短歌 あかね』の中から私にとって印象的だった百首を選び紹介しています。光子が詠んだ日本語の短歌に、辛菜穂子さんの翻訳による英語短歌が加わって新たな魅力が加わっています。

続く「第二部 春日光子の生涯」では、短歌が詠まれた背景がわかるよう、光子の人生を文章と写真で紹介しています。

Tanka by Akane.

 The first section of this book, *100 Selected Tanka*, introduces a selection of Mitsuko's most powerful tanka. These tanka were translated into English from the original Japanese by poet Naoko Shin, who used her poetic skills to breathe new life into Akane's words. The second part of this book, *The Life of Mitsuko Kasuga*, introduces the life of Mitsuko, providing more context to Akane's tanka.

 Each tanka in this book holds in it the essence of one woman's life. I trust you'll delight in the beauty of tanka crafted by a first-generation Japanese in Mexico who lived a bold life.

 この本に収められたそれぞれの歌には、一人の女性の人生が凝縮されています。メキシコでたくましく生き抜いた日系一世の、味わい深い短歌の世界をお楽しみください。

MESSAGE FOR THE ENGLISH EDITION
刊行によせて

Carlos Tsuyoshi Kasuga Osaka
春日 カルロス剛

I hope this book will be enjoyed by readers trying to challenge themselves in new fields. Much can be learned from the lives of immigrants who transcend borders and challenge themselves to thrive in foreign societies.

My mother Mitsuko had a pioneering spirit. She was strong-willed and would often say, "I will not be defeated." She worked harder than anyone else I know and had the vitality needed to turn difficult moments into opportunities.

My mother's life was so difficult that it required her to be exceedingly strong to keep from despairing at life's challenges. As a young woman, she left her family in Japan and traveled by herself to Mexico. During World War

　これは、新しいフィールドに挑戦しようとするすべての人に読んでもらいたい本です。国境を越えて挑戦を続けた移民たちの生き様は、私たちに多くのことを教えてくれます。
　今は亡き私の母・光子は、開拓精神にあふれていました。気が強く、「負けるもんか」が口癖でした。誰よりもよく働きました。ピンチをチャンスに変えるバイタリティーを持っていました。裏を返すと、母の人生は、強気で立ち向かっていかなれば自分が吹き飛ばされてしまいそうになるほど、つらく厳しいものだったとも言えます。母は22歳でふるさと日本の家族から離れて、一人メキシコにやってきました。第二次世界大戦中には、「敵国人」としてメキシコ国内での強制移住を経験。さらに58歳のときに、夫（私の父）が早世してしまいます。しかし幾多の困難にもくじけることなく、母はメキシコの地で私たち六人の子どもを育て上げました。何事にも人一倍の努力を惜しまない人でした。
　母が遺した短歌を私が初めて読んだのは、2014年に「あかね」がスペイン語訳と

II, she experienced forced migration within Mexico because she was a "citizen of an enemy country." Furthermore, she became a widow when she was only 58 years old because her husband (my father) died at an early age. Despite the numerous difficulties she faced, she overcame them to raise her six children in Mexico. And she never lamented having to work twice as hard to ensure her family's wellbeing.

The first time I read my mother's tanka was in 2014 when Akane's book was translated into Spanish. Reading her tanka allowed me to appreciate how the wonder and beauty of the world can be found in everyday life.

It is said that the difference between ordinary and extra*ordinary* is that little *extra*. Without a doubt my mother had that kind of extra. Despite knowing her all my life, I was truly impressed by her intense spirit and poetic efforts. Ironically, my mother never strived for an extraordinary life. However, she did live every moment of her daily life intensely. Thus, her tanka expresses the inherent beauty of an ordinary life.

The reason my mother's tanka touches so many people is likely because

---

してまとめられてからのことです。短歌を読んで、私ははっとさせられました。この世の中の尊さ、美しさは、日常の中にこそ息づいているものなのだということに気づいたのです。

　extraordinary(非凡) と ordinary (平凡)を分けるのは、エクストラだといいます。母には間違いなくそのエクストラがありました。過剰なまでの根性と努力に、私はいつも感嘆の念を抱いていました。しかし、歌の中にあったのは、むしろ美しくも平凡(ordinary)な毎日でした。母は決して、非凡な人生を生きようと思って毎日を暮らしていた (strive for extraordinary lives) わけではありません。ただただ、日常の中の瞬間瞬間を精一杯生き抜いていたのです。

　母・光子の短歌が多くの人の心に響くのは、光子がある意味ではありふれた一人の女性にすぎないから、なのかもしれません。光子のとことん個人的な思いや経験が詠み込まれているからこそ、その短歌はかえって普遍性をもち、時代の確かな息づかいが感じられるものとなったのです。短歌の中に詠み込まれている母の人生は、

刊行によせて　MESSAGE FOR THE ENGLISH EDITION

Mitsuko was simply a woman who lived her life to the fullest. My mother's life, as expressed through her tanka, speaks not only to Japanese immigrants living in Mexico, but also to other immigrants around the world. Her poems reflect not only the lives of immigrants, but also the experiences of all people living in an unfamiliar world.

Since we are born in a time of rapid change, sometimes we need to force ourselves to stop, look around, and take a deep breath. I feel that in my mother's tanka we can find essential hints on how to slow down and keep perspective in today's fast-moving world.

メキシコの日系人だけでなく、世界中の移民たちとも共通するものがあります。また移民でなくとも、自分の知らない世界へと飛び出して挑戦を続ける、すべての人につながるものがあります。

　変化の激しい時代を生きる私たちですが、時には立ち止まって振り返り、深呼吸をすることも必要です。母・光子の短歌の中に、今を生きる私たちにこそ大切なヒントがあるように感じています。

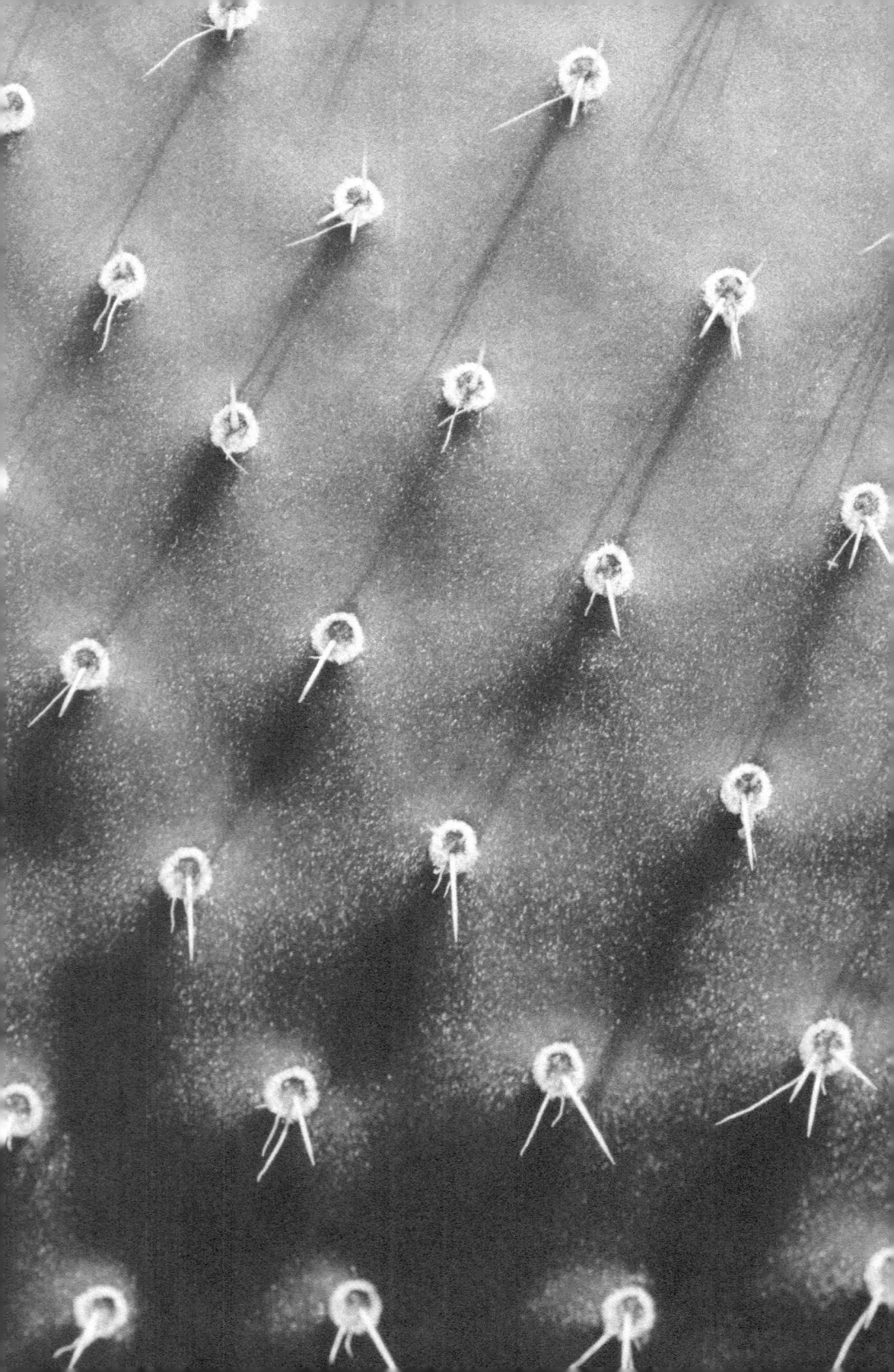

Part I
100 Selected Tanka

第一部
短歌百選

**English Tanka Translation:
Naoko Shin**

英語短歌:辛 菜穂子

**Spanish Tanka Translation:
Cynthia Viveros Cano**

スペイン語短歌:シンティア・ビベロス

14 PART I 第一部

LEGEND
凡例

A: Context of Tanka (*Kotobagaki*)　ことばがき 詞書
B: English Tanka　英語短歌
C: Original Japanese Tanka　日本語 短歌
D: Spanish Tanka　スペイン語 短歌
E: Interpretation in Japanese　日本語口語訳

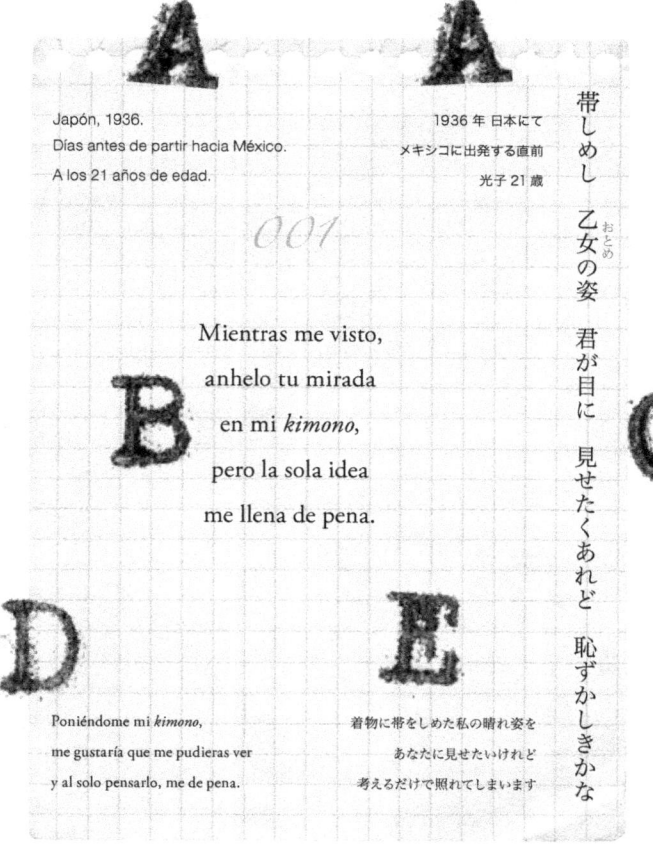

I. CROSSING THE OCEAN
海をわたる

II. MY CHILDREN
子への思い

III. MY HUSBAND
夫への思い

IV. ADAPTED SPIRIT, PERSISTENT VALUES
揺れる心、変わらぬ信念

V. DAILY LIFE
暮らしの中で

VI. MY LAND
ふるさと

VII. MY GRANDCHILDREN
孫への思い

VIII. WITHOUT YOU
夫 遠く

Japan, 1936.
Just before leaving Japan for Mexico.
At the age of 21-22.

1936 年 日本にて
メキシコに出発する直前
光子 21 〜 22 歳

my maiden form
cinched in this *obi*,
I long for you to see me-
I think about it
and I blush.

Mientras me visto,
anhelo tu mirada
en mi *kimono*,
pero la sola idea
me llena de pena.

着物に帯をしめた
私の晴れ姿を
あなたに
見せたいけれど
考えるだけで照れてしまいます

帯しめし 乙女（おとめ）の姿 君が目に 見せたくあれど 恥ずかしきかな

あかね 短歌百選　100 SELECTED TANKA　17

across
distant seas,
paving my own way-
a great duty
to fulfill.

Del otro lado
de los mares lejanos,
veo los caminos
en los cuales he de andar
para alcanzar mi visión.

はるかな海のみちを
こえて行くのだ
私の人生の道の
大きな務めを
はたすために

八重の潮路　越えて行くべし　我が道の　大きつとめを　果さむとして

I. CROSSING THE OCEAN
海をわたる

II. MY CHILDREN
子への思い

III. MY HUSBAND
夫への思い

IV. ADAPTED SPIRIT, PERSISTENT VALUES
揺れる心、変わらぬ信念

V. DAILY LIFE
暮らしの中で

VI. MY LAND
ふるさと

VII. MY GRANDCHILDREN
孫への思い

VIII. WITHOUT YOU
夫 逝く

Mitsuko around 31 years old. 光子31歳ごろ

ten years ago
I married this man.
we are poor,
yet my five children
fill my heart.

Hace diez años
que vine a esta tierra
para casarme.
Pobre, pero cinco hijos
llenan días de alegría.

嫁いできて
10年が経った
貧しいけれども
五人の子どもたちに
満ち足りた気持ちになる今日の日

嫁ぎ来て　十年経にけり　貧しくも　五人の子らに　心満つ今日

I am already
a woman in my thirties.
my sole and earnest
hopes for my children
only continue to grow.

Soy una mujer
Ya con más de treinta años.
Pienso en mis hijos.
Para ellos, ilusiones
Sólo siguen creciendo.

女の私も
30代になり
ひたすら
わが子に望むことが
多くなって

我(われ)をみな三十路(みそじ)を経(へ)れば ひたすらに 吾子(あこ)に望めること 多くして

1948, Mitsuko 34 years old.　　　　1948年　光子34歳

sixth child,
I will soon be your mother.
this morning
I sensed your stirrings,
my heart still in awe.

Del sexto niño,　　　　　　　　　六人目の子の
ya casi seré madre.　　　　　　　母になろうとしている
Esta mañana,　　　　　　　　　今朝になって
sentir sus movimientos　　　　　胎動を感じ
logra asombrar mi alma.　　　　おごそかな気持になる

六人目の　母ならむとす　今朝にして　胎動を感ず　心おごそか

my six children
have six distinct shades
of character.
in their contradictions
I am content.

Yo, con seis hijos,
veo el mundo de seis formas.
Con pros y contras,
diferentes, cada una
satisface al corazón.

六人の
子どもがいると六とおりの
性格があって
長短ひっくるめて
心が満たされる

六人の　子があれば六いろの　性(さが)ありて　その長短(ちょうたん)に　心満(み)ちゆく

"do not give in!"
reflecting on the good and the bad
of these words
I feel regret,
yet I utter them once more.

"¡Nunca te dejes!",
parte bueno, parte no.
Mientras lo digo,
reflexiono y decido
repetirlo a mis hijos.

「負けるな」と
子どもに言葉をかけることの
善し悪しを
反省しつつも
ついまた同じことを言ってしまう

「負けるな」と　云う言の葉の　善し悪しを　反省しつゝ　されど又云う

with these
gnarled hands
our six
children were nurtured.
I admire my hands.

Miro mis manos,
parecen acabadas.
Aquellas mismas
a mis hijos cuidaron.
Puedo verlas, bellas son.

節くれだった
私のこの手によって
六人の
子どもが育っているのだと思い
自分の手をいとおしく見つめる

節（ふし）高き　我のこの手に　六人の　子が育ちおり　いとしみ見るも

"wrong again, Mamá!"
my children correct me
as I rehearse my "L".
in the end I get lost
between "L" and "R".

"¡Te equivocaste!"
nuevamente mis hijos,
mientras practico,
cuando escuchan mi "L".
No distingo "L" de "R".

「また、だめ」と
わが子に言われて
「L」と発音し直すのだけれど
そのうちついに「L」と「R」の
違いがわからなくなってしまう

「またダメ」と吾子に云はれて「L」と云へどついに「L」と「R」と分らなくなる

At Choapan #5 1942-1952.　　チョアパン 5 にて　1942〜1952 年
Mitsuko 28-38 years old.　　　　　　　　　　　光子 28〜38 歳

the children
return with tadpoles.
"we can keep them
in our tub," they announce,
but well over one hundred.

Vuelven mis hijos,
renacuajos cautivos
que traen para criar
en la tina del baño,
pero son más de un ciento.

おたまじゃくしを
子どもたちがとってきて
浴槽で
飼おうよと言うけれど
その数100匹以上

おたまじゃくし　子等(ら)は取り来て　浴槽(よくそう)に　飼(か)へと云(い)へども　百匹余り

in our home
resides a longstanding guest,
this turtle.
our little children call her
Kameko Kasuga.

Esa tortuga,
viviendo años en casa.
Y mis chiquitos
la llaman por su nombre,
es Kameko Kasuga.

我が家に
長く住んでいる
カメなので
春日カメ子と
幼い子は呼ぶ

我が家に 永く住みたる カメなれば カメコカスガと 幼子は云う

no one can hear us
nor judge us.
our six children,
my husband and I
speak of their wonders.

Yo con mi esposo,
no hay preocupaciones,
nadie escucha.
Sobre cada hijo hablamos,
sobre sus maravillas.

誰(た)にはばかる　こともなければ　六人の　子の特長を　夫(つま)と語りぬ

誰かに気がねする
必要もないので
六人の
子どものいいところを
思う存分夫と語り合う

my son
grows strong with
my husband's traits.
my heart swells
as I help with his shoes.

Corazón pleno,
con sus zapatos
calzo a mi niño.
De mi esposo ha heredado
el mismo buen carácter.

我が夫の　長所を享けて　育つ子に　心満ちつゝ　靴はかせやる

私の夫の
長所を受け継いで
育つ子どもに
満ち足りた気分で
靴を履かせてやる

At Choapan #5.
Mitsuko 37 – 38 years old.

1952年　チョアパン 5 にて
光子 37 〜 38 歳

an autumn night—
I sit in on a debate
among my children.
this may be a happiness
only a parent knows.

Noche de otoño,
en medio de mis hijos
que charlan y discuten.
Tan solo privilegio
de madre, esta alegría.

秋の夜
子どもたちが議論している
輪の中に私はいる
これは親だけが知る
幸せかもしれない

秋の夜を　子等の議論の　中にゐつ　親のみが知る　幸かも知れず

1954. En Martí #126.
A los 39-40 años de edad.

1954年　マルティ126にて
光子39〜40歳

German children
march together with
ours.
I intently follow
their small, black heads.

Mis hijos, niños
entre los alemanes,
los miro marchar.
Y yo soy quien les cuida,
sus cabecitas negras.

ドイツ人の
子どもたちに交じって行進する
わが子の
黒い頭を
私は見守る

ドイツ人の　子等(ら)と行進する吾子(あこ)の　黒き頭を　我は見守る

1954. En Martí #126.　　　1954 年　マルティ 126 にて
A los 39-40 años de edad.　　　　光子 39 〜 40 歳

in a circle
with my children,
our stained hands
continue to shell
tender walnuts.

Con mis hijos, yo　　　　子どもたちと一緒に
en medio de un círculo　　　輪になって座り
vamos abriendo　　　　　手を黒く染めながら
las nueces de castilla.　　　まだ柔らかい
Manos ennegrecidas.　　　クルミを割り続ける

子等と共に　車座になり　手を染めて　まだやわらかき　胡桃割りつぐ

my son has grown
to knot his necktie
with grace.
the sight of his broad shoulders
delights me.

Aprendieron ya
mis hijos a ponerse
sus corbatas. ¡Ah!
La vista de sus hombros,
fuente de felicidad.

ネクタイを
上手にしめられるほど
子どもが成長した
そのがっしりした肩を見るのさえも
私にはうれしい

ネクタイを　上手にしめる　子となりぬ　肩幅さえも　我に嬉しく

under the garden sun,
plums dry as I reminisce
about my distant child.
the parrot squawks
his name.

ecando chamoy
bajo el sol, pienso: mi hijo
que lejos estás.
De pronto una voz fuerte
grita tu nombre. ¡Loro!

遠き子を　思ひつゝ梅を　干す庭に　鸚鵡は高く　吾子の名を呼ぶ

遠く離れて暮らす子を
思いながら梅を
干している庭で
オウムが甲高い声で
その子の名前を呼ぶ

1965. At Martí #126.
Mitsuko 50-51 years old.

1965年　マルティ126にて
光子 50〜51歳

for seven years
I have faithfully planted
this flower.
now I await my returning child,
finished with studies abroad.

Planté esta mata
en el jardín, cada año
estos siete años,
espero el retorno del
hijo que estudia fuera.

毎年同じ草花を
庭に植え続けて
7年間の
留学を終えて
帰ってくる子を待っている

草花を　庭に植えつぎ　七年の　留学卒えて　帰る子を待つ

a rainy night—
I wait for my tired daughter
to return home,
a pot of *pozole* soup
simmering over the fire.

Noche de lluvia,
a la olla de pozole
fuego le prendo,
para mi hija, que llega
agotada del día.

雨の夜を　疲れて帰る　吾娘の為　ポソレの鍋の　火をもやし待つ

雨の夜
疲れて帰ってくる
娘のために
ポソレの入った鍋を
火にかけて待つ

027

grandchild in my arms,
I stand by the gate
waiting for letters
from my distant children,
wondering, where from today?

Mi nieto en brazos,
espero en la entrada.
Hago una pausa.
¿Llegará el día de hoy
por fin carta de mi hija?

孫を抱きながら
戸口にずっと立って
遠くに住む子どもからの
手紙を待っているのだ
今日はどこから届くだろう

孫抱きて　門に立ちつぎ　遠き子の　手紙待つなり　今日は何所から

today
I sent my daughter
to study abroad.
now I am a mother
who counts the days to her return.

Al extranjero
mandé a mi hija a estudiar.
Hoy, soy la madre
que está contando días
hasta su vuelta a casa.

留学に
行く娘を送り出した
今日からは
帰る日を指折り数える
母となる私

留学に　行く娘送りぬ　今日よりは　帰る日数う　母となる我

July 1972.. Culiacán.	1972年6月　クリアカンにて
With Esperanza Mazako	エスペランサ真佐子ら夫婦が働く
and her husband.	カキの養殖所を見学
Mitsuko 58 years old.	光子 58 歳

in the estuary
they labor,
covered in mud.
my children's business
will, I hope, bear fruit.

En el estero
en el lodo, a mis hijos
veo trabajar.
Y anticipo cuando
sus esfuerzos den frutos.

エステロ（淡水湖）で
泥まみれになって
働いている
子どもたちの仕事が
実を結ぶ日を待ち望む

エステロに　泥にまみれて　働ける　子等（ら）の仕事の　実る日を待つ

1982. Washington D.C.,
Mitsuko 68 years old.

1982 年　ワシントン D.C. にて
光子 68 歳

one lime
costs five pesos
in Potomac
where my daughter resides.
she longs for Mexico.

En el Potomac
muy cerca de Washington
radica mi hija.
Cinco pesos por limón,
nostalgia de México.

ライム一個が
メキシコのおかねに換算して五ペソもする
ワシントン近郊ポトマックに
娘は住んでいて
メキシコを恋しく思うらしい

レモン一ケ　墨貨五ペソの　ポトマクに　娘は住みながら　メヒコ恋うらし

1984. Mazatlán.
Mitsuko 70 years old.

1984年　マサトランにて
光子 70 歳

when they call
I fly to them.
my aging body
bends to my children.
I am at peace.

Caigo en cuenta que
yo voy si me lo piden.
Cuando a mis hijos
hago caso, se infunde
de paz mi viejo cuerpo.

頼まれれば
飛んでいく私か
年老いた身を
子どもに任せてついてゆけば
安らかな気持ちに包まれる

頼まれゝば　とび行く我か　老いの身を　子に従へば　安けさの裡

at the carnival,
I dance
with the people of Mexico.
in this photograph
I look nothing like 70.

Foto, Mazatlán.
Bailo en el carnaval
entre mexicanos.
Y por nada de nada
parezco de setenta.

カーニバルで
メキシコの人たちと
踊っている
写真の中の私は
とても70歳とは思えない

カーニバルに メヒコの人等(ら)と 踊りいる 写真の我は 七〇ならず

crew of women
with strong, burly arms—
I am here, too.
our work begins
packing shrimp.

Sentada en medio,
doñas fuertes, sus brazos
a cada lado.
Y ya empiezo a trabajar
empacando camarón.

腕の太くたくましい
女たちの中に
私もいて
エビを箱に詰める
作業を始めた

腕太き　女衆の中に　我もいて　エビ箱詰めの　作業始めぬ

just now
eyes of the prawns
all turn to me
the moment I reach
and twist off a head.

Todos los ojos,
todos los camarones
me están mirando,
justo al levantar uno
para decapitarlo.

エビの目が
みんな私のほうを向く
今まさに
頭をもぎ取ろうと
手で触ったその瞬間

エビの目が　みなわれに向く　今まさに　頭をもぐと　手をふれし時

I. CROSSING THE OCEAN
海をわたる

II. MY CHILDREN
子への思い

III. MY HUSBAND
夫への思い

IV. ADAPTED SPIRIT, PERSISTENT VALUES
桐てる心、変わらぬ信念

V. DAILY LIFE
暮らしの中で

VI. MY LAND
ふるさと

VII. MY GRANDCHILDREN
孫への思い

VIII. WITHOUT YOU
夫 逝く

1954, Mitsuko 40 years old.   1954 年　光子 40 歳

our flaws
we've come to accept,
each in the other.
we've lived 18 years together
to arrive at this day.

Dieciocho años,
los hemos compartido.
Perdonándos,
cada uno nuestras faltas,
para llegar hasta hoy.

欠点は
互いに許し
合いながら
ともに18年を
生きて今日があるのだ

欠点は　互に許し合ひながら　十八年を　生きて今日があり

030

at times
I feel annoyed,
but at all times
I know this me would not exist
without my husband.

A veces pienso
que te odio, pero siempre
he sabido que
de no haberte tenido
no sería la que soy.

或る時は　憎しと思う　こともあれど　夫なくて在る　我とは思はず

時には
憎らしいと思う
こともあるけれど
夫なくてる存在する
私とは思わない

my husband's hand
was so warm
that night
walking over grass wet with evening dew
under a crescent moon.

Noche de luna,
mientras que nuestros pasos
van sobre el rocío
de la yerba del jardín,
tus manos me abrigan.

夫の手は
温かかった
三日月の夜
露に濡れている庭の
草を踏みながら歩くとき

夫の手は　あたたかかりき　三日月の　庭の夜露の　草を踏む時

I. CROSSING THE OCEAN
海をわたる

II. MY CHILDREN
子への思い

III. MY HUSBAND
夫への思い

IV. ADAPTED SPIRIT, PEERSISTENT VALUES
揺れる心、変わらぬ信念

V. DAILY LIFE
暮らしの中で

VI. MY LAND
ふるさと

VII. MY GRANDCHILDREN
孫への思い

VIII. WITHOUT YOU
夫 逝く

they all
describe me as
cheerful.
that I may be but
I, too, have tears.

Dice la gente
que soy alegre y que
tengo energía.
Pero yo sé bien, tengo
también mis lágrimas.

人はみんな
私を評して
朗らかな人だと
言うけれど
そんな私にも涙はあるのだ

人は皆　我を評(ひょう)して　朗(ほが)らかな　人と云(い)へども　我に涙あり

033

I defied everyone
when I crossed that ocean,
so it can't be helped.
when I am in pain,
I accept my circumstances.

Al cruzar el mar,
contra lo que decía
mi gente allá,
ora puedo decirme:
¡Haz lo que tienes que hacer!

人の反対を押し切って
海を渡ってきた
その結果なのだから仕方ないと
悲しい時は
自分に言い聞かせる

人に背(そむ)き　海を渡りし　そが為(ため)と　悲しき時は　自らあきらむ

I have nothing
to embellish my appearance
but this frame of mind,
to collect inner truths
and live on.

Sin los adornos
que se llevan por fuera,
concentrada estoy
en vivir sin mentiras
dentro de mi corazón.

外見を飾るものは
何もない
心して
内に偽りない真心を
ためて生きよう

外に飾る　何物もなし　心して　内なる誠(まこと)　ためて生きなむ

those who can
crudely express
their feelings;
I feel envy,
I feel pity.

感情を　露骨に現わしうる人を　うらやみてみつ　憐れみてみつ

感情を
あからさまに表現
できる人のことを
うらやましく思ってみたり
かわいそうに思ってみたり

Gente que deja
profundos sentimientos
a todos saber,
les tengo un poco envidia
y otro poco tristeza.

they talk as if
possessions
are proof of success.
I avoid such folks
and drink my tea.

Aquellos que creen
que al tener más cosas
son exitosos,
lejos de mi corazón.
Yo prefiero tomar té.

物を所有していることを
ただ成功の
証のように言う
人を自分の心から遠ざけて
私はお茶を飲む

物持つを 只成功の 如く云う 人を心に さけて茶を飲む

1954. Mitsuko 40 years old, She opened the house and received 86 students at *Tacubaya Gakuen*.

1954 年　家を開放し
86 名の生徒とともに
タクバヤ学園を始める
光子 40 歳

I shall swallow
my unspoken words,
though I am
deliberately slandered
in this article before me.

言挙げで　耐えて行くべし　ことさらに　我を誹謗の　記事は見つれど

Yo me contengo,
y no llego a palabras.
Esa noticia
que me llena de insultos
ha llegado a mi vista.

言い立てないで
耐えていこう
とりたてて
私の悪口を言う
記事が目に入ってはくるけれど

1954 or after.
At Martí #126.
Mitsuko 40 years old.

1954 年以後
マルティ126 にて
光子 40 歳

a handful
of tanka I have never shared,
held in secret.
living my forties fervently,
I am a woman!

Sin revelarlos,
aquellos mis poemas,
nadie conoce,
incluso a mis cuarenta.
¡Soy tan sólo una mujer!

世には発表しない
短歌をいくつか
密かに持ちながら
四十代を生きよう
ああ私はひとりの女なのだ

世に出さぬ　歌の幾首を　秘め持ちて　四十路を生きむ　女我はも

love is
a sin, they say
in my mountain country.
I can't help but
carry this regret.

Tierra mía haces
Pecado del romance
¡Es una pena!
Si todavía llevo
uno en mis entrañas.

恋愛することは
罪だと言うような
山国に育って
今となってはどうしようもない
心残りを持ち続けている

恋愛を　罪の如云う　山国に　育ちて返らぬ　悔を持ちつぐ

from here,
how should I live?
by discovering
my own limitations
I can see myself.

A partir de ahora,
¿cómo debe uno vivir?
Límites propios,
claramente entendidos,
sin perderme de vista.

これからは
どのように生きるべきだろうか
自らの
限界を知って
自己を見つめる

これよりは　如何に生くべき　自らの　限界を知れば　自己を見つむる

1975. Mitsuko 61 years old. 　　　1975年　光子61歳

flags of
Mexico and Japan
placed proudly
atop the factory roof:
"Here are *Nikkei*!"

Pongo a volar
banderas en el techo:
México-Japón.
　La fábrica anuncia, que
　"Sí, así es, ¡aquí hay *nikkei*s!"

メキシコと
日本の旗を
力強く立てて
「ここに日系あり」と
見せる工場の屋根

メキシコと　日本の旗　打ち立てゝ　日系在りと　工場の屋根

1976. Mitsuko 62 years old.   1976 年　光子 62 歳

"you immigrant!"
though they scorn us,
we carry
with pride a spirit
that is pure.

Ojos que gritan:
¡Pinches inmigrantes! No vean,
Mejor díganlo.
Al fin, nuestro espíritu
es pureza y nobleza.

「移民ども」と見下して
　言うならば言うがよい
　　　　魂の
　誇り高く清らかなものを
　私たちは持っているのだ

移民共と　云うならば云へ　魂の　潔らけきもの　我等持つなり

disingenuous beings
crowd the world
we live in.
the path of the golden mean
is not for me.

不信の人　数多き世に　生き行けど　中庸の道は　我は行くまじ

誠実でない人が
数多くいる世の中に
生きているけれど
中庸の道は
私は行かない

Vivo en un mundo
con gente deshonesta
y otra confiada.
No ando el camino medio
sino el propio camino.

1980. Mitsuko 66 years old.   1980年　光子66歳

moxa burns on
my foot's acupoint.
I remember, these feet
supported me in Mexico
to stand here today.

Masaje a mis pies,
es gracias a ustedes que
llegué hasta aquí.
Gracias a estos pies estoy
parada hoy en México.

足の「三里のツボ」に
灸をすえながら思う
この足に
支えられながらメキシコの大地に
今存在している私のことを

三里の灸　すえつゝ思う　この足によりてメヒコに　今在る我を

I. CROSSING THE OCEAN
海をわたる

II. MY CHILDREN
子への思い

III. MY HUSBAND
夫への思い

IV. ADAPTED SPIRIT, PERSISTENT VALUES
隠れる心、変わらぬ信念

V. DAILY LIFE
暮らしの中で

VI. MY LAND
ふるさと

VII. MY GRANDCHILDREN
孫への思い

VIII. WITHOUT YOU
夫逝く

Mitsuko in her 20s.

光子 20 代

a sales clerk
presents the fabric
for which I reach.
seeing my chapped hands,
I swiftly hide them.

Entre mis manos
pone la señorita
una muestra de tela.
Veloz, ya las escondo,
mis manos tan gastadas.

店員が
見せてくれている布地に
手を伸ばし持ったが
荒れている手が恥ずかしくて
急いで隠した

店員の　示せる布地　持つ我の　荒れしその手を　急ぎかくしぬ

あかね 短歌百選　100 SELECTED TANKA　65

At Chapango #5,
Mitsuko 37-38 years old.

チョアパン5にて
光子37〜38歳

テンガステ　マルチャンティータと　云う声を　聞きたく今日も　ノパル買いおり

"marchantita,
tenga usted!"
voices in the market
I want to hear today,
so again I shop for *nopales*.

Para escucharlas
"¡Tenga usted marchantita!"
esas palabras.
También el día de hoy
voy a comprar nopales.

「はいどうぞ、
お客さん！」
と言う声を
聞きたくて今日も
食用サボテンを買っている

In the garden,
Mitsuko was growing Japanese
vegetables and herbs.

光子は庭でカラシナ
などの日本の野菜を
大切に育てていた

too dear
for the *miso* soup,
left unpicked,
mustard greens bloom.
this morning, butterflies dancing.

Sin desperdiciar
karashina en sopa,
en *misoshiru*,
florece en el jardín
con una mariposa.

味噌汁に
入れるのがもったいなくて
摘まないでおいた
カラシナが花を咲かせて
今朝はそこで蝶が舞っている

味噌汁に　入るを惜しみて　摘まざりし　辛子菜咲けば　今朝蝶が舞う

1954, at Martí #126.
Mitsuko 39-40 years old.

1954 年　マルティ 126 にて
光子 39 〜 40 歳

女人さえ　宇宙をかける　時来たり　今より生まる　人の世を想う

even women
fly to space.
such an era has arrived.
I dream the world
of those born hereafter.

Llegó una era
en que hasta las mujeres
van al espacio.
Mundos de aquellos por nacer,
ya imagino.

女性までもが
宇宙飛行をする
時代が来た
これから生まれてくる
人の世界に思いを馳せる

I have spent days
with this tanka,
scattered and unformed.
it rains
without a hint of clearing.

Pasan varios días
y mis canciones quedan
sin lograr forma.
Días en qué la borrasca
el sol desdibuja.

うまくまとまらない
短歌にこだわりを残したまま
ここ数日を
過ごしている私である
雨空もずっと晴れないままだ

まとまらぬ　歌にこだわる　幾日を　過ごす我なり　雨も晴れざる

ウィツゥラコチ　かぼちゃの花の　ケサディーヤ　愛(め)でてメヒコの　人となり行(ゆ)く

quesadillas of
squash blossom and
huitlacoche
are my special favorite.
I am becoming Mexican.

Mis favoritas
son esas quesadillas
de huitlacoche y flor.
Son ellas que me hacen
más y más mexicana.

ウィトゥラコチェや
カボチャの花が入った
ケサディージャを
愛するようになって私もメキシコの
人となっていく

1972. Mitsuko 58 years old.
She would dig bamboo shoots
every spring

1972 年　光子 58 歳
春に土から顔を出す
タケノコは懐かしい
日本の味だった

today in our garden
I dig for bamboo
with my daughter-in-law.
even the tough outer skins
are ingredients for *sushi*.

Hoy, yo y mi nuera
takenoko del jardín
cosechamos.
Para cocinar hasta
los brotes delicados.

庭に出てきた
竹の子を嫁と
一緒に今日掘って
皮の柔らかいところまで余さず
寿司の具にする

我が庭の　竹の子嫁と　今日掘りて　姫皮までも　すしの具となす

1983. Mitsuko 69 years old.

1983年　光子 69 歳
[さなぶり：田植えのあと神に感謝し
ともに働いた人をねぎらう農村の行事]

with talk of the
Sanaburi ritual and the like
my daughter-in-law and I
share our hometown
in the kitchen, preparing *miso* paste.

さなぶりの　話などして　同郷の　嫁と厨に　味噌仕込みする

Platico con mi nuera,
festival de *Sanaburi*,
de Ina, somos dos.
Juntas en la cocina
mientras hacemos *miso*.

さなぶりの
話などをしながら
同じ信州出身の
嫁と一緒に台所で
味噌の仕込みをする

over sixty years
I have lived
in Mexico,
the flavors of ginger flower *miso* soup
move me to tears.

El *misoshiru*,
sabores de jengibre.
Llena de lágrimas
ya más de 60 años
que estoy aquí en México.

メキシコで
もう60年余り
暮らしている私を
泣かせるのだ花みょうがの
味噌汁の懐かしい味は

メキシコに　六十余年　在る我を　泣かすみょうがの　子の味噌汁は

I. CROSSING THE OCEAN
海をわたる

II. MY CHILDREN
子への思い

III. MY HUSBAND
夫への思い

IV. ADAPTED SPIRIT, PERSISTENT VALUES
慣れる心、変わらぬ信念

V. DAILY LIFE
暮らしの中で

VI. MY LAND
ふるさと

VII. MY GRANDCHILDREN
孫への思い

VIII. WITHOUT YOU
夫 逝く

1951. In Tacubaya.
Mitsuko 37-38 years old.

1951年　タクバヤにて
光子 37〜38 歳

the sounds
of my steps on ice,
so crisp.
feeling nostalgic,
I continued walking all the way.

Escucho al pisar
el agua congelada,
esos recuerdos,
de memoria lejana.
Sigo camino en ella.

さくさくと
氷を踏むと
その音が
懐かしく感じられて
そのまま歩き続けた

さくさくと　氷を踏めば　その音の　なつかしきまま　歩みつづけぬ

September 1962. 48 years old. Mitsuko returned to Japan for the first time in 27 years.

1962年9月
日本に27年ぶりに帰国
光子48歳

I return
to the hometown
I have not beheld for twenty-seven years.
I accompany
my father, painfully aged.

二十七年　相見ぬ故郷に　帰り来て　いたく老いたる　父に従う

Observo mi hogar
tras veintisiete años
sin un vistazo.
Le hago caso a mi padre,
allí ha envejecido.

27年間
目にすることがかなわなかった故郷に
帰ってきて
ぐっと老いた
父につき従う

he persevered
through a changing world.
I wash
my father's back,
holding back tears.

変わる世を　生き耐えて来し　父の背を　洗ひてやりぬ　涙こらえて

No se ha rendido
por dolor ni tristeza
en un mundo que cambia.
Su espalda tallo, padre,
me quedo mis lágrimas.

変わる世の中を
耐えて生き抜いてきた
父の背中を
洗ってやった
涙をこらえながら

proof of
a long family tradition, my grandmother
took pride in
this moss-covered *kaya*.
Now I lean on its trunk.

El árbol prueba,
orgullo de mi abuela,
familias nobles.
Bello musgo tupido,
me recargo en la kaya.

「代々続く立派な家の
証だよ」と祖母が
誇りにしていた
苔むすカヤの木の
太い幹に私はよって立つ

古き家の　証と祖母が　誇りたる　苔むす榧の　幹に倚り立つ

* kaya is a slow-growing tree native to Japan. Its yellow-gold wood is prized for the construction of Go boards and Shogi boards.

nostalgia
it is not, but
when the florist
carries cosmos,
I inadvertently stop to buy them.

郷愁と　云うにあらねど　コスモスの　花屋にあれば　寄りて買い行く

Si encuentro cosmos,
no es que extrañe el terruño,
pero me acerco.
Y por no sé que azares
al florista los compro.

ふるさとが恋しいから
というわけでもないのだけれど
コスモスが
花屋にあるとつい
寄って買い求める

May 10, 1972.
Mitsuko's father passed away.
Mitsuko was 57 years old.

1972年5月10日
光子の父、永眠する
光子57歳

I stare
at the single point where
the sun sets in the sea.
father and mother are gone,
my hometown ever distant.

海に日の 沈む一点を 見つめゐき 父母既に亡き 故郷は遠し

En aquel punto
donde se pone el sol,
está mi tierra,
allá lejos, mis padres
no me están esperando.

海に日が
沈むその一点を
見つめていた
父母が既に亡くなってしまった
故郷ははるか遠い

letters to
my hometown
are dwindling.
now that Father is gone,
what ought I write?

Cartas que escribo,
ya son cada vez menos
las que iban rumbo a mi hogar.
Al perder a mi padre
ya no sé que contarles.

ふるさとへ
送る手紙の数が
減っていった
父が亡くなった今
何を書けばいいというのだろう

ふるさとへ　手紙の数は　減り行きぬ　父の亡き今　何を書くべき

the aroma of mulberry
permeates the cocoonery.
my mother, feeding new leaf,
was so youthful,
so beautiful.

Olor de *kuwa*
inunda todo el cuarto.
Es la comida
del gusano de seda.
Joven, bella, mi madre.

桑の葉の
匂いたつ部屋で
蚕にえさをやる
母は若かった
美しかった

桑の香のたつ蚕室に給桑の母若かりし美しかりし

calling out,
"Lord Silkworm," my mother was
devoted to
silk cultivation.
from this way of life
I have learned.

Gusanos santos,
como decía mi madre,
gusanos de seda.
Esmeros para crecer
mucho aprendí de ese actuar.

お蚕様と　云いて養蚕に　はげみたる　母の姿に　我は学びし

「お蚕さま」と
大切に呼びながら
養蚕に励んでいた
母の姿から
私は学んだ

1980. Mitsuko 65 years old.　　　　1980 年　光子 65 歳

this *yae-zakura*,
transplanted
from Japan,
now blooming in Mexico,
filled with infinite clusters.

Planté y creció
aquel *sakura* que
traje de Japón.
Son racimos sus flores
aún insisten en crecer.

遠く日本から
運ばれ植えられた
八重桜が
メキシコで咲いた
花房を幾重にも重ねて

日本ゆ　移植されたる　八重ざくら　メヒコに咲きぬ　房を重ねて

* *yaezakura* means multi-layered cherry blossom and is a symbol of strength, as compared to the delicate *sakura* like *somei yoshino*.

yae-zakura
buds picked and pickled
in brine,
that day,
my mother was within me.

Para salarlos,
botones de cerezo
un día recogí.
Hacía aquello y al tiempo
mi madre me habitaba.

八重桜の
つぼみを摘んで
塩漬けにした
あの日私の中には
私の母がいた

八重ざくらの　つぼみをつみて　漬けたりき　かの日は我に　母が有りたり

1984. Mitsuko 70 years old.

1984 年　光子 70 歳

おてんばと　云はれながらも　竹馬に　乗りて遊びし　ふるさとの庭

tomboy,
they call me,
but I still
play on stilts
in my hometown garden.

Donde yo anduve
en mis zancos de bambú,
el mismo jardín.
Allí donde me decían:
¡Mira que vivaz eres!

おてんば娘だと
言われながらも
竹馬に
乗って遊んだ
ふるさとの庭

I. CROSSING THE OCEAN
海をわたる

II. MY CHILDREN
子への思い

III. MY HUSBAND
夫への思い

IV. ADAPTED SPIRIT, PERSISTENT VALUES
揺れる心、変わらぬ信念

V. DAILY LIFE
暮らしの中で

VI. MY LAND
ふるさと

VII. MY GRANDCHILDREN
孫への思い

VIII. WITHOUT YOU
夫 逝く

1963. Mitsuko's first grandchild,
Miki Yamazaki, was born.
Mitsuko was 49 years old.

1963 年
初孫・山崎美希生まれる
光子 49 歳

this morning
a fragrant breeze.
the birth was registered.
From today, Miki, too,
is una Mexicana.

風薫る　朝に届出　すませたり　今日より美希も　メヒコの一人

Una mañana,
vientos y suave aroma
con Miki al volver.
Dice el registro civil,
una mexicana más.

さわやかな風が吹きわたる
朝出生の届け出を
すませた
今日から美希も
メキシコの一人

067

my hopes
will be carried in Mexico
through you.
as I hold my grandchild,
her warmth envelops me.

"Heredarás
sueños para México".
Se lo murmuro.
La idea abraza a mi nieto,
su calidez me envuelve.

我が願(ねが)い メヒコにつぎて 行く汝(なれ)と 孫を抱(いだ)けば ぬくみつたい来(く)

「私の願いを
メキシコに受け継いで
いくきみなのだ」と
思いながら孫を抱くと
そのぬくもりが伝わってきた

1964. Mitsuko's second grandchild, Maki Yamazaki, was born. Mitsuko was 50 years old.

1964 年
第二の孫山崎真希生まれる
光子 50 歳

when young,
I sang to my children
"hato-po-po."
now I sing to my grandchildren,
days of peace.

我若く　吾子に歌いし　ハトポッポ　孫に歌いて　安らぎの日々

Joven, cantaba
canciones a mis hijos.
De nuevo canto.
Ahora, para mis nietos,
son de paz todos los días.

私が若いときに
自分の子どもに歌ってやった
「ハトポッポ」の童謡
孫のために歌って
安らぎの日々

I sun-dry plums
for my distant children
and grandchildren.
I rest my hands and
gaze at the plane passing above.

De secar chamoy
mis manos ya descansan,
hijos y nietos,
es para los de lejos
cruza en el cielo un avión.

遠くに住む子どもと
孫にやろうと思って
梅を干している
その手を休めて
空を横切る飛行機を見つめる

遠き子と　孫にやらむと　干す梅の　手を休めつゝ　過ぐ機見つむる

1964.
Bought a house at Iztaccíhuatl #72.
Mitsuko 50 years old.

1964年
イスタシワトル72に家を買う
光子 50歳

070

this autumn day—
sewing a layette
inside a warm room.
my daughters-in-law
are plump and content.

秋の日の　ぬくき室ぬち　産着縫う　嫁等の姿　ふくよかにして

Cuarto de otoño.
Para mi nieto, cosen
primeras prendas.
mis nueras calientitas
robustas y felices.

秋の日の
暖かい部屋の中で
産着を縫っている
嫁たちの姿は
ふっくらと満ち足りている

071

my grandchild
attends kindergarten
and learns by heart
the national anthem of Mexico.
I want to sing with you.

Ya van al kinder,
ya mis nietos aprenden
su himno nacional.
¡Vamos a cantar juntos,
cantemos abuelita!

幼稚園へ
通っている孫が
覚えてくる
メキシコの国歌
きみと一緒に歌おう

幼稚園へ　通へる孫が　覚え来る　メヒコの国歌　汝と歌はむ

1975. Mitsuko 61 years old.　　　　　1975 年　光子 61 歳

years from now
the grandmother you will remember
is me.
when I recall this,
I am mindful of my words.

年経ちて　汝が思い出す　祖母我と　思う時言葉　慎みて云う

Años pasarán
yo seré tu recuerdo:
soy la abuelita.
El trato con mis nietos,
cuidadosas palabras.

年月が経った時
きみが思い出す
祖母はこの私なのだと思う時
自分の言葉に気をつけて
孫に声をかける

1977. Mitsuko 62 years old.   1977年　光子62歳

"Grandma,
come quick, look!
ume pickle flowers
are blooming!"
my young grandchild exults.

Dice mi nieto:
Abuelita ven a ver,
dice el pequeño.
Hay flores en el árbol,
el de chamoy japonés.

「おばあちゃん、
こっちに来て見てごらん
梅干しの
花が咲いた」
と幼い孫が言う

おばあちゃん　来て見てごらん　梅干しの　花が咲いたと　幼孫云う

1982. Mitsuko 68 years old. 　　　1982年　光子68歳

a tanka
not coming together.
perhaps impatient,
I hurl harsh words
at my grandchildren.

¿Estoy enfadada
por no rimar mis versos?
Puede que lo esté
 a mi nieto le dije
unas palabras bruscas.

短歌の一首さえも
まとめられなくて
焦っているからだろうか
孫に対して荒っぽい
言葉をぶつけてしまう

歌一首　まとめえぬ今日の　あせりにか　孫には荒き　言葉を放つ

a child of the sea,
my grandson drew
a lobster
looking as if it could
spring forth from its plate.

Una langosta
dibujo de mi nieto,
el que es costeño.
Casi salta del plato
y se sale el dibujo.

海の町で育つ
孫が描いた
伊勢エビは
今にも皿の上から
飛び出してきそうだ

海の子の　孫が描(か)きたる　いせえびは　皿の上より　はね出(い)ずる如(ごと)

1984. Mitsuko 69 years old.　　　　　1984年　光子69歳

I crouch
and receive kisses from
my grandchildren.
they encircle me.
I am already nearing seventy.

Estoy agachada,
besos de mis nietos
llenan mi cara
y casi estoy yo por cumplir
unos setenta años.

かがんでは
キスを受けながら
こうやって孫たちに
囲まれて私ももう70歳に
近くなったのだなあ

かゞみては　キスを受けつゝ　孫たちに　囲まれ七〇に　近き我かな

my grandchildren
are taller and sturdier
than I.
they surround me.
"Ay, Grandma!"

Mis nietos ahora
más altos y más fuertes,
todos mis nietos.
Me rodean y me dicen:
"¡Ay, Obaachan... ay, Obaachan!"

私よりも
背が高くがっしりした
孫たちが
私を囲んで言う
「ああ、もう、おばあちゃんったら!」

我よりも　背高く太き　孫たちが　われを囲みて　「アイ！おばあちゃん」

I. CROSSING THE OCEAN
海をわたる

II. MY CHILDREN
子への思い

III. MY HUSBAND
夫への思い

IV. ADAPTED SPIRIT, PERSISTENT VALUES
揺れる心、変わらぬ信念

V. DAILY LIFE
暮らしの中で

VI. MY LAND
ふるさと

VII. MY GRANDCHILDREN
孫への思い

VIII. SIN TÍ
夫 逝く

March 1973.
Tsutomu Kasuga died from pancreatitis
at the age of 62.
Mitsuko was 58 years old.

1973年3月
急性すい炎にて62歳の夫
春日カルロス勉が急逝
光子58歳

078

he worked
and worked to the end.
my husband's hand
is already cold,
powerless.

Entre mis manos,
las manos de mi esposo
más trabajo y más.
Ahora, manos frías
ahora, manos sin fuerza.

働きに
働いて逝ってしまった
夫の手は
既に冷たい
既に力がない

働きて 働きて 逝きし 夫の手の 既に冷たし 既に力なし

079

if I cried
out loud, my heart
would ease.
I know this, yet I cannot cry
as a spring day passes.

大声に　泣かば心も　安らぐと　思へど泣けず　春の日は逝く

Pena corazón.
Tal vez llorar a gritos
bajaría el dolor.
Aún sin llanto, pasó el día
sin vuelta. Primavera.

大声で
泣いたなら心も
少しは安らぐだろうと
思うけれど私は泣けなくて
春日は逝ってしまった

*"a spring day" carries double meanings as her husband's family name "Kasuga" literally means "spring"+"day."

May 1973. Mitsuko buries the ashes of Tsutomu in Ina, Japan. She was 58 years old.

1973年5月　亡夫の遺骨を伊那市美篤の丘へ埋葬した　光子58歳

for my husband,
who sleeps beneath the
giant cypress tree,
come across the valley, *hototogisu*,
and sing.

大ひばの許に眠れる夫のため子規鳴け谷渡り来て

Duerme mi esposo
debajo de un gran árbol,
pájaro cucú.
En su nombre, crúzalo,
el valle, llora a gritos.

大きなヒバの
木の下に眠っている
夫のために
ホトトギスよ鳴いてくれ
谷を渡って来て鳴いてくれ

*the *hototogisu*'s passionate chirp is often reffered to as sound of "coughing up blood" and represents deep sadness in Japan.

the dull
ache in my bones
is more distinct today.
now that my husband is gone,
I must bear it alone.

しんしんと 骨の疼きの しるき日よ 夫のなき今 一人堪ゆべし

Incluso días que
hasta duelen los huesos,
los aguanto sola.
Ya sin mi esposo, aguanto
todo con mi soledad.

しんしんと
骨の痛みの
激しい日よ
夫がいなくなってしまった今
一人で堪えなければ

April 1974.
In Zihuatanejo.
Mitsuko 59 years old.

1974年4月
シワタネホにて
光子59歳

I often followed
behind my husband
at this beach.
Now I cannot find his footprints
and I grieve.

Vuelvo a la playa
donde seguí sus pasos
hace varios años.
Mas ya no están sus huellas.
mundo, colmas tristeza.

以前夫の後に
ついて散歩した
砂浜にやって来たが
夫の足跡はもう
どこにもなくてたまらなく悲しくなる

夫の後　従い行きし　砂浜に　その足跡の　無くてなげくも

088

a giant wave
breaks on the shore.
in that fleeting moment,
I heard my husband's joy
surging forth.

Gran ola rompe
el instante en la orilla
y me parece...
...que acabo de escuchar
su grito de alegría.

巨大な波が
岸に当たってくだけた
　　　その瞬間
　　夫の歓声が
湧いて聞こえた気がした

巨(おお)き波　岸にくだけし　たまゆらに　夫(つま)の歓声　湧(わ)きし心地す

1974. The 2nd *Obon* after Tsutomu's death. Mitsuko 59 years old.

1974 年　夫が他界してから
二度目のお盆を迎える
光子 59 歳

"during *Obon*,
Grandpa will return,"
I tell them.
our assembled grandchildren
cheer with delight.

お盆には　おぢいちゃんが来ると　我云えば　集へる孫等　歓声を挙ぐ

Dije a mis nietos:
"En *obon*, vuelve Ojiichan".
Todos gritaron.
Muchos gritos de alegría,
porque ya va a regresar.

「お盆になれば、
亡くなったおじいちゃんがくるんだよ」
と私が言うと
集まっていた孫たちは
無邪気に歓声をあげた

once again,
my grandson's voice
on the phone.
"Grandpa
isn't there yet?"

おぢいちゃんは　まだ来ないのと　外孫の　電話の声の　しきりなりけり

Por teléfono
me pregunta mi nieto
que vive lejos:
"¿Y todavía no llega?"
"¿Aún no ha llegado Ojiichan?"

「おぢいちゃんは
まだ来ないの」と
離れて暮らす孫から
たびたび電話が
かかってくる

"When Grandpa
returns, let's try to
keep him,"
one grandchild proposes,
and another nods.

Dice: "En este *obon*,
cuando llegue Ojiichan
haremos algo".
"Sí, para que se quede",
dicen mis otros nietos.

「お盆におじいちゃんが帰ってきたら
　もう行ってしまわないように
　　　しましょう」と
　　言い出す孫と
　　うなずく孫と

おぢいちゃんが　行かないように　しませうと　言い出ずる孫と　頷く孫と

During *Obon* festival, some make "spirit horses" using vegitables so that the spirit of ancestors can ride.

故人の精霊が馬などに乗って早く帰って来るようにという願いをこめて野菜で動物の形を作り供える日本のお盆の習慣

ride these
horses made of
eggplants and cucumbers.
please come home, my late husband.
the grandchildren are waiting.

Con los caballos
que te hicimos cruza y ven
del otro mundo.
Berenjena y pepino,
eso fue lo que usamos.

ナスで作った馬
キュウリで作った馬に
乗ってお越しください
あの世の夫よ
孫たちの待つ家へと来てください

茄子の馬　キューリの馬に　乗り給い　参らせよ亡き夫　孫の待つ家へ

1974. Mitsuko 59 years old.   1974 年　光子 59 歳

someday,
a day to cry
to my heart's content.
will it truly come?
I've endured without tears.

Todos los días, hasta hoy
me aguanto las lágrimas
todas, por siempre.
¿Algún día lloraré hasta
que no pueda llorar más?

いつの日か
気がすむまで思いきり
泣ける日が
私にも来るのだろうか
泣かずにじっと耐えてきて

何時の日か　心ゆくまで　泣ける日の　我にもあるか　泣かず耐え来て

089

a cold wave is coming
the weather forecast
reports.
snow will blanket Mount Popo
where my husband sleeps.

Una ola de frío
anuncian las noticias.
¿Nieve en el Popo?
Lugar donde descansa
aquel, mi esposo amado.

寒波来と　テレビニュースは　伝えたり　夫ゐるポポは　雪降りてゐむ

寒波が来ると
テレビニュースは
伝えた
夫が眠るポポカテペトル山では
雪が降り積もっていることだろう

March 9th, 1975. 60 years old.
The second anniversary of
Tsutomu's death. At Mt. Popocatépetl.

1975年3月9日　夫の三年忌を
　　　　　　ポポカテペトル山にて行う
　　　　　　　　　　　　光子60歳

feeling
this vast distance
between life and death
my hand grips
a piece of my husband's bone.

Aquí en mi puño
apretando cenizas,
cuerpo de mi amor.
La distancia entre vida
y muerte es infinita.

果てしなく広がる
生と死の間の距離を
　感じながら
夫の骨のかけらを
手のひらに握りしめる

茫々と　生死の距離の　あるところ　夫の骨片　掌に握りしむ

clothes and shoes
preserved as they were
when he was here.
I have awaited my
late husband's return for three years.

Ropa y zapatos,
como cuando aún vivía,
justo en su lugar.
Ya pasaron tres años,
anhelos, vuelve mi amor.

衣も靴も　在りし日のまゝ　保ちゐて　亡夫帰る日を　三年待ちたり

服も靴も
生きていたときのまま
大切にもって
夫が帰ってくる日を
もう3年待った

several times
played for a fool,
my husband's sorrow
was never spoken.
he took this to his grave.

Viviste engaños,
con tristes sentimientos,
y varias veces.
Te fuiste al otro mundo
sin nunca compartirlos.

何度か
人にだまされながらも
悲しみを
人には言わないまま
あの世に旅立ってしまった夫よ

幾度か　騙されながら　悲しみを　人には云はず　逝きし亡夫はも

his dreams
continue to be fulfilled.
our children and I
transcend
the cruelty of others.

Mis hijos y yo,
la crueldad de la gente,
Sobrevivimos.
Capaces de continuar
empresas de mi esposo.

今は亡き夫の夢を
実現することができた
子どもと私は共に
つらい人の世を
生き抜いてきて

亡夫(つま)の遺志(いし) 貫(つらぬ)き得たり 子と我と 辛き人らの 中を生き来て

preparing this land,
let the sound of the
bulldozer's engine
reach the peaks of Mount Popo
to announce the construction.

Máquinas, ruido.
La construcción del *Liceo*.
Aplanar tierra.
Que retumben los ecos
hasta el Popo, donde estás.

整地する
ブルドーザーの
エンジンの
音よ届け
ポポカテペトルの嶺まで

整地する　ブルドーザーの　エンジンの　音もとゞけよ　ポポの高嶺に

1974. Mitsuko 64 years old.　　　　　1979 年　光子 64 歳

even in dreams
my beloved husband does not visit.
still I yearn,
a widow for six years.
I live this reality.

No me visitas
siquiera en sueños.
¡Te extraño mi amor!
Si bien me quedé sola,
seis años de realidad.

夢にさえ
出てきてくれない亡き夫を
今もなお恋しく思いつつ
寡婦となってから6年の時が流れた
この現実を生きる

夢にさえ　出で来ぬ亡夫を　尚恋いて　寡婦六年の　現実に生く

time passes
like the flow of water;
it slips quietly by.
on those who remain
jacaranda blossoms fall.

Cauce del tiempo
fluyes, pasas como agua.
Los que no han muerto,
para ellos todavía caen
flores de jacaranda.

年月は
流れる水のように
過ぎてゆき
死なずに残った者の上に
ハカランダの花が散る

歳月は　水の如くに　過ぎ行きて　遺りし者に　ハカランダ散る

1984. Mitsuko 70 years old.　　　　1984年　光子70歳

unfinished,
two bottles of my husband's
medicine.
twelve years have drifted by
since I set them aside.

Tengo dos frascos,
su medicina
aún por acabar.
Se la sigo guardando
desde hace 12 años.

飲みかけの
夫の薬の
瓶が二つ
それを取っておいて
12年がたつ

のみかけの　夫(つま)の薬の　瓶(びん)二つ　そをとりおきて　十二年たつ

horses made of
eggplants and cucumbers
have shriveled
again during this *Obon*.
he did not return after all.

Esos caballos
que te iban a recoger
ya se marchitan.
Berenjena y pepino.
No llegas, aunque esperé.

夫を迎えるために
ナスやキュウリで作った馬も
しぼみ始めてしまった
今年のお盆にも
ついに夫は帰って来なかった

茄子の馬　キューリの馬も　なえばみて　今年の盆も　遂に夫来ず

099

directly facing
the peak of Mount Popo,
cosmos
cover this hill.
I've chosen my burial place.

ポポの嶺を　真向かひにして　コスモスの　咲きみつ丘を　墓地ときめたり

Con vista al Popo
cosmos florecen sin fin,
lo he decidido.
Sí, aquí, éste es el monte
donde estará mi tumba.

夫が眠るポポカテペトル山を
正面にのぞんで
コスモスの花が
いっぱいに咲いている丘を
私の墓地と決めた

1979. Mitsuko 64 years old.　　　1979年　光子64歳

firmly rooted
in Mexico, our children
will live on.
when my husband beckons me
I will recount it all.

Los hijos nuestros,
con raíces en México,
todos florecen.
Quiero contarle a mi amor
cuando vaya a su lado.

「子どもたちはメキシコで
　たくましく根を張り
　生きていますよ」と
死んだ夫に招かれて天国に
行ったときには語って聞かせよう

メキシコに　根強く子等は　生き行くと　亡夫に召されし　日には語らむ

あかね 短歌百選　100 SELECTED TANKA

BIOGRAPHY I
略歴 I

English Tanka Translation: Naoko Shin
英語 短歌　辛 菜穂子

Naoko Shin, originally from Tokyo, Japan, is a freelance writer and translator. Her past projects include copy writing for website redesign, and interpreting for production and advertising agencies working with Japan. She enjoys reading a wide range of books, from fiction to poetry, from design thinking to children's books. Naoko is passionate about words, and their ability to move others through stories and poetry. Currently, she resides in the Bay Area with her husband and daughter who both share her love of words.

東京出身。フリーランスのライター、翻訳家、詩人。ウェブサイトのコピーライティング、製作会社や広告代理店の翻訳・通訳の分野で活躍。読書が好きで、小説から詩、デザイン思考、童話まで幅広いジャンルをカバーする。物語や詩として人の心を打つ「ことば」の力に魅了されている。現在は夫、娘とともにサンフランシスコ・ベイエリア在住。

あかね 短歌百選　100 SELECTED TANKA　125

Spanish Tanka Translation: Cynthia Viveros Cano
スペイン語 短歌　シンティア・ビベロス

(D.F., México, 1975)
Cynthia Viveros Cano studied International Relations at el Colegio de México and has a Master's degree in Public Policy from Duke University. She works at the United Nations in New York and has lived in Colombia and Brazil. Avid reader of poetry. One day, she had chance to read Akane's tanka, and recreated the tanka in Spanish. Now her favorite poets are Pessoa, Amichai and Issa.

メキシコの大学コレヒオ・デ・メヒコで国際関係を学んだ後、アメリカのデューク大学で公共政策の修士号を取る。ニューヨークの国連本部に勤務。コロンビア、ブラジルへの赴任も経験する。
文学好きのシンティア・ビベロスはある時、あかねの短歌をスペイン語に訳した原稿を偶然読んで感銘を受け、音韻を大切にしたスペイン語の短歌として再構築する試みを自発的に始め、それが本書出版のきっかけとなった。
敬愛する詩人は、フェルナンド・ペソア（ポルトガル）、イェフダ・アミハイ（イスラエル）、小林一茶（日本）。

1975年、メキシコシティー生まれ。

Compilation / Interpretation: Aiko Chikaba
選歌 / 解釈　近葉 愛子

[The biography of Aiko Chikaba is at the end of the Part II.]

[プロフィールは第二部末尾を参照]

Part II

THE LIFE OF MITSUKO KASUGA

第二部
春日光子の生涯

Text: Aiko Chikaba

文：近葉 愛子

English Tanka Translation: Naoko Shin

英語短歌：辛 菜穂子

MAP
地図

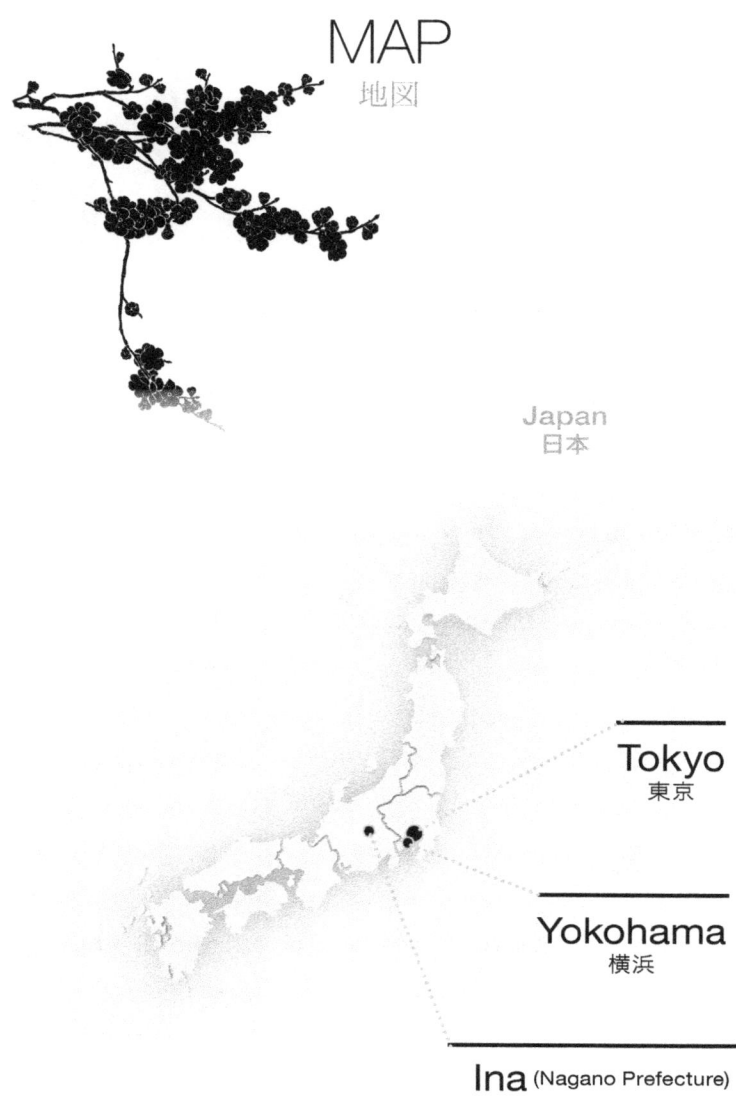

Japan
日本

Tokyo
東京

Yokohama
横浜

Ina (Nagano Prefecture)
伊那（長野県）

春日光子の生涯　LA VIDA DE MITSUKO KASUGA

PART II 第二部

1. A JAPANESE GIRL WITH AN AMBITIOUS SPIRIT

Tanka 061, 062, 065

信州育ちの勝ち気な娘

春日光子の生涯　THE LIFE OF MITSUKO KASUGA

Mitsuko was born to Inao and Yukie Osaka on June 15, 1914 in the city of Ina, Nagano. She was the second of four sisters. With her parents busy growing rice and breeding silkworms, she was cared for by her grandparents, who adored her but were very strict. Their home opened onto vast rice fields, beyond which she could see the imposing Mount Komagatake. Mitsuko's childhood elapsed, casual and carefree, in this idyllic natural setting.

Little would young Mitsuko know that she would one day leave her homeland for a faraway land, where she would find success as a tanka poet after a lifetime of weathering misfortunes and overcoming struggles. Yet despite the physical distance that would eventually separate Mitsuko from the home of her youth, it remained evident in her tanka, which bore the imprint of Ina's sunsets and the auburn glow that glistened off Mount Komagatake at dusk. Her pen

Mitsuko (on the right) and her sisters
姉たちと光子（右）

1914年（大正3年）6月15日、光子は小坂伊那雄とゆきえの子として、長野県の伊那で産声をあげた。四人姉妹の二番目である。両親は家業の稲作と養蚕で忙しく、代わりに同居する祖父母によく世話をされたが、しつけは厳しかった。家の前には田畑が広がり、周囲を取り囲む野山のその向こうには駒ヶ岳がそびえ立つ。そんな豊かな自然の中で、光子は子ども時代をのびのびと過ごした。

のちに光子はこの故郷を離れ、遠い異国の地で逆境にたえながら歌人として花を咲かせるのだが、そんな人生を歩むことになることなど、子ども時代の光子には知る由もない。しかし、ふるさと伊那の空に広がる夕焼けや、茜色に染まる駒ヶ岳は、歌人としての光子の原風景だった。40歳になってから名乗った雅号「あかね」には、彼女のふるさとへの思いが込められていた。

光子は姉妹の中でも特に好奇心旺盛で、家の外で自転車を乗り回したり竹馬で遊んだりするのが好きだった。そんな光子も、12歳になって伊那高等女学校に通うことになる。そこで光子は修学旅行の一環として横浜港から神戸まで一等客船に乗るという、思いがけない体

name, Akane, adopted when she was 40 years old, referred to that deep red glow and embodied her feelings for her hometown.

Mitsuko was a curious girl who liked to try new things, from biking to ice skating. Her interest in the world around her also made her an avid reader of classic Japanese books and an engaged student. At the age of 12, Mitsuko enrolled in the Ina School of Secondary Education for Girls. Her school's principal, Teisuke Yagi, was a pioneering educator who believed that even the children from farming villages should set their sights on the vast outside world. During a school trip, Mitsuko had the good fortune of travelling on a first class passenger ship from Yokohama Bay to Kobe. Normally this grand ship traveled on routes to Europe, so it was unlike anything students from the Japanese countryside could have ever imagined. It was this experience that first led Mitsuko to dream of the world across the sea.

Mitsuko's mother—Yukie Osaka
母・ゆきえ

験をした。先進的な教育者だった校長の八木貞助が、農村の生徒たちも広い世界に目を向けるべきだと考えて取り計らったものだった。その大型客船は、通常はヨーロッパ航路を航行しているもので、山国育ちの生徒たちの目にはあまりにまぶしかった。この体験がきっかけで、光子は海の向こうの世界に憧れを抱くようになったのである。

　しかし、穏やかに暮らしていた光子の一家は突然、不幸に見舞われる。父・伊那雄が出納係を務めていた養蚕組合で、部下が組合の資金を持って芸者と駆け落ちし、行方不明になるという事件が起こったのだ。職責を重く受けとめた伊那雄は、部下の不祥事の責任をとり、私財を投げ打って弁済することになった。一家はたちまち落ちぶれ、貧乏な暮らしを余儀なくされた。しかし、生活の困窮以上に光子を深く傷つけたのは、村の人々の態度が冷たくなったことだった。光子14歳のときである。

　悪いことは続くもので、その翌年には母・ゆきえが病気のため若くして亡くなる。度重なる不幸に見舞われ、光子は悲しみに打ちひしがれた。

　それまで光子は、高等女学校を終えた後も進学を希望していたのだが、家庭の状況を考え

Two years later, Mitsuko's peaceful family life was devastated by misfortune. One of her father's subordinates at the silkworm breeders' union, where Inao served as treasurer, stole the union's money to run off with a geisha. Feeling a deep sense of responsibility for his subordinate's misdeed, Inao used his own money to reimburse the union. This sunk the Osaka family into poverty. However, what hurt the family more than their new circumstances, was the callous disregard with which the villagers began to treat them.

Things only seemed to get worse for the Osaka family from there. The following year, Mitsuko's mother, Yukie, became sick and passed away. Overwhelmed by the ongoing misfortune, Mitsuko was devastated.

Mitsuko had wanted to continue her

Mitsuko's father—Inao Osaka
父・伊那雄

ければ断念せざるを得なかった。さりとて、働いて家計を支えようにも、今では考えられないほど男女格差が大きい当時の社会では、女性が高給の仕事につくことは容易ではない。さらに1929年にはアメリカを震源地として世界恐慌がスタート。そのあおりをうけて海外市場で生糸が売れなくなり、養蚕業に多くを頼っていた信州の地域経済全体が落ち込んだ時期でもあった。

かといって、結婚という選択も光子には難しかった。当時の農村女性の結婚適齢期は十八歳ぐらいとされていたが、結婚しようにも家には資産がない。花嫁道具や持参金が用意できなければ、嫁ぎ先の家での立場が低くなってしまうのは目に見えている。自分の人生をそんなふうに台無しにするのはまっぴらである。光子には、家に残って農業をする道しか残されていなかった。

「今に見ていろ」。光子は悔しさをぐっと押し殺し、毎日汗と泥にまみれて働いた。十七歳の、青春というにはあまりにつらい日々だった。

1931年、満州事変が勃発。光子が住んでいた伊那の町からも、多くの男性が中国大陸の

education beyond secondary school, but her family's new situation forced her to give up this dream. Furthermore, the disparity between men and women's pay was so great at the time that it was hard to find a job that paid enough for Mitsuko to help support her family. In addition, the Great Depression took place in 1929, originated in the United States. Because of that, the sales of silk in the oversea market were decreasing. Thus, the regional economy of Nagano, which had been relying hugely on sericulture industry, slowed down as well.

The option of marriage also proved to be a difficult one for Mitsuko. At the time, eighteen was considered the ideal age for women to marry, but marriage was unlikely for a young woman from a family without assets. Mitsuko knew that without the ability to provide the bridal furniture and dowry, she would have a low status in the family she married into. Because she refused to waste her life that way,

Mitsuko cropping rice
稲刈りをする光子

戦地へと旅立っていった。伊那の女子青年団長になった光子は、出征の見送りをしたり、戦地に慰問袋を送ったりすることに、かろうじて生きがいを見出していた。

春日光子の生涯   THE LIFE OF MITSUKO KASUGA   135

the only option left for Mitsuko was to remain with her family and work on the family farm.

Mitsuko worked through mud and sweat, determined to overcome her family's misfortunes. The trials of life already weighed heavily on her seventeen-year-old shoulders.

After the Manchurian Incident of 1931, which led to armed conflicts between Japan and China, many men from Mitsuko's town left to join the battle in mainland China. As the leader of the Ina Girls' Youth Group, Mitsuko found a sense of purpose in sending care packages to their young men on the battlefront.

Mitsuko's original home (on the left)
光子が育った家 (左)

2. BECOMING A "PICTURE BRIDE"

Tanka 001, 002

「写真花嫁」

春日光子の生涯   THE LIFE OF MITSUKO KASUGA

Today it seems impossible to imagine a young woman in Japan being willing to set sail across the ocean to become a bride in a faraway country after seeing a single photo. And yet, that was what Mitsuko did.

When Mitsuko was 21 years old, a matchmaker came to her father with a photo of a potential suitor. The young man in the photo was Tsutomu Kasuga. Also from Ina, he was the seventh of nine siblings. Mitsuko didn't know him because he had left for Mexico five years before.

According to the matchmaker, Tsutomu's father had been a successful businessman who not only was a major landowner in Ina and a real estate developer in Tokyo, he was also involved in shortwave radio manufacturing. The Kasuga family had been wealthy, able to send four of Tsutomu's brothers to study in the United States. However, Tsutomu's father had become ill and died in his fifties, leading to a quick downturn in the family's fortune. Crop sharers had revolted

Tsutomu left Japan at the age of 20
20歳の若さで日本を後にした春日勉

たった1枚の写真を見ただけで、遠い異国の地に花嫁として旅立つ女性が、現代の日本にいるだろうか？

光子が21歳を迎えたある日、父・伊那雄のところに見合い写真を携えた仲人がやってきた。写真の青年は春日勉。光子と同じ伊那の出身で、九人兄弟の七番目。5年ほど前に単身メキシコに渡ったのだという。

仲人によると、勉の父はもともと伊那の大地主であり、加えて短波ラジオの製造や東京での不動産開発を手がけるなど、やり手の実業家でもあった。家は裕福で、勉の兄たち四人はアメリカに留学したほどであった。ところが勉の父が、病をわずらい五十代で早世。父の死後、小作農たちの反乱が起きて土地が失われたうえ、商売も傾いて一家には借金ができた。ただちに経済的に自立することを迫られた勉は、希望していた医学部への進学やアメリカ留学をあきらめ、中等学校卒業と同時に地元の伊那電鉄に就職。車掌や整備士として休まず働いたらしい。兄弟が力を合わせて稼いだ甲斐あって、やがて春日一家の負債整理にめどが立つ。勉はその時点で、より大きなチャンスを求めてメキシコに渡ることを決めたという。

and occupied his land and his other business also failed in his absence. With his family in debt, Tsutomu gave up plans to enter medical school or study in the United States, and instead started working for the local Ina Railway Company as soon as he graduated from middle school. He worked tirelessly as a conductor and mechanic and, along with his brothers, was able to settle the family's debt. At that point, Tsutomu traveled to Mexico seeking better opportunities.

Mitsuko was intrigued by Tsutomu Kasuga's marriage offer. In addition to being able to empathize with his experience of loss, she felt that the young man in the photo exuded a sense of integrity. Her father, Inao, also approved

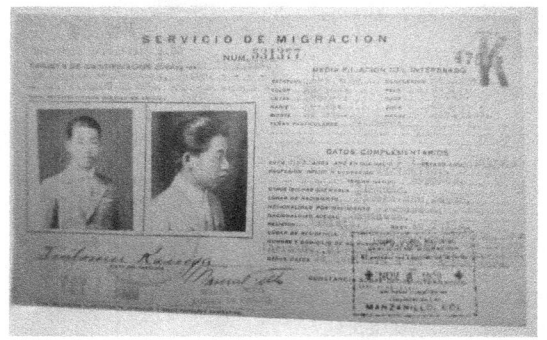

Tsutomu Kasuga's document
春日勉　メキシコ移住の記録

　光子はこの縁談に興味をひかれた。写真の青年からは、誠実そうな人柄がにじみ出ている。親が他界し進学をあきらめざるをえなかったという、自分に似た境遇にも共感を覚えた。
　父の伊那雄もこの縁談に賛成だった。青年の実家のある美篶という村は、光子たちの住む小沢から10キロメートル足らずの距離である。伊那雄は養蚕組合の仕事を通じて春日家の人々とも面識があり、メキシコに移住した勉の熱心な働きぶりも耳にしていたのであった。
　それにしても、花婿候補が評判の良い働き者の男だからといって、愛娘を地球の反対側に嫁がせるものだろうか。一つ思い当たるのは、伊那雄が昔抱いていた夢である。伊那雄は若い頃、港町・横浜に暮らしていた時期があり、ハワイへの移住に興味を持っていた。しかし、長男であったため信州の実家に戻らねばならず、移住の希望は叶わなかった。父は、自らの夢を娘の光子に託そうと思ったのかもしれない。
　見合い写真だけでの結婚には、当時の日本人移民の特殊事情もあった。メキシコへ移住した者の多くは独身男性で、若い女性はほとんどいなかった。そのため、永住を決意した男性が日本人女性と家庭を築きたいと思っても、周りに結婚相手がいないという問題があった。毎日の生活費を稼ぐのが精一杯という暮らしをしている移民男性には、日本に帰って相手を

of the proposal. Since the Kasuga family was from Misuzu, a village a mere ten kilometers (six miles) away, Inao knew of them through his work with the silkworm breeders' union, and was aware of Tsutomu's reputation as a hard worker.

However, even if Tsutomu was a great marriage candidate for Mitsuko, could a father send his daughter halfway around the world to wed a man neither knew personally? What swayed the family in favor of the match was the memory of Inao's own youthful dreams. During his youth, Inao had spent a period of time living in the port town of Yokohama and had even considered moving to Hawaii. However, as the eldest son, he had the

Tsutomu working in Mexico
(second left with a rifle)
メキシコで働き始めた頃の勉
（左から二人目のライフルを持っている男性）

見つけるだけのお金もなければ、時間もない。そこで、故郷の親戚などを仲立ちにして、日本に住む女性と写真や手紙を交換する「お見合い」がよく行われていた。日本に住む両家の親同士が会って話をし、縁談がまとまったら日本で籍を入れるのである。こうすれば、嫁いでゆく女性たちはメキシコ在住の夫の「呼び寄せ」という形でビザを取って、単身メキシコに渡ることができるようになる。これを「写真結婚」といい、嫁いでゆく女性たちは「写真花嫁」と呼ばれていた。光子の中学校の同級生にも、この「写真結婚」でペルーやブラジルに渡った女性たちがいた。

とは言え、写真と手紙でしか知らない男性と結婚するため太平洋を越えるというのは、きわめて勇気のいることだった。しかし光子は、新天地を求めてメキシコへ渡ることを決めた。

「母が若くして亡くなってしまったので、あんな無鉄砲ができたのかもしれない」と、のちに光子は語っている。

1936年5月。れんげの咲く田んぼと残雪光る駒ヶ岳の美しさを胸に刻み付け、光子はふるさと信州を離れた。家を出る前に、苔むすカヤの大木にしがみついて、別れの言葉を告げ

obligation to return to the family home in Nagano, so his dream of migrating had never come to pass. Perhaps Mitsuko was meant to fulfill Inao's dreams.

"Picture marriages" came about as a response to the patterns of Japanese migration of the time. For instance, the vast majority of Japanese migrants in Mexico were single young men, so suitable marriage partners were scarce. These migrant Japanese men, who had to work very hard simply to make enough money to subsist, had no money or time to return to Japan to find a bride. Because of this situation, relatives back home had to play the role of matchmaker, exchanging their photos and letters with women living in Japan. Parents living in Japan would meet, and if a marriage agreement was

Wedding ceremony without groom
新郎のいない結婚式

た。「私はもう戻ることがないかもしれません。どうか私の家族を守ってください。」光子の大好きな祖母が、「この大きな木は代々続く立派な家の証拠だよ」と言って大切にしていた思い出の木である。

伊那から横浜の港までは、姉が光子に付き添った。いわゆる「写真結婚」だったので、このとき光子は既に戸籍上、春日勉の妻「春日光子」に変わっていた。見ず知らずの人のところへ嫁ぐわけだから、不安がないわけではない。しかし、「春日勉さんは、九人兄弟の中でも一番の親孝行者」という仲人の言葉を頼りに、「それならきっと、妻や子どもにもやさしくする人にちがいない」と信じた。いや、信じるしかなかったのである。

光子が荷物として持っていたのは、たった二回分の着替えと日の丸の旗。あとは、数十冊にのぼる日本語の本だけである。横浜に着いた光子は、山崎米、藤沢みすずという女性たちと合流した。彼女たちもまた、光子と同様「写真結婚」でメキシコに向かう仲間である。三人の花嫁は船に乗り込み、再び帰れるかどうかわからない日本に別れを告げた。

楽洋丸と名付けられたその船は、チリのバルパライソ航路の貨物船だった。船には中南米

struck, the marriage would be registered in Japan and the bride would get a visa and travel to Mexico alone. These arrangements were called "picture marriages" and women who married in this fashion were referred to as "picture brides." Among Mitsuko's secondary school classmates, there were girls who traveled to Peru and Brazil as picture brides.

Despite there being a logistical and economic need for picture brides to travel overseas by themselves, Japanese society during this period was hardly accepting of women traveling abroad alone. Braving social disapproval, Mitsuko decided to travel to Mexico alone in search of a better life. When asked, years later, what drove her to accept Tsutomu's proposal and face

Mitsuko and her sisters
花嫁衣装を着た光子と姉妹

へ向かう日本人移民が、光子たちの他にも何人も乗りこんでいた。その移住先はメキシコの他、ペルー、ボリビア、パラグアイ、アルゼンチンなどさまざまだった。

　船上で光子は、本を読んで時間を過ごした。船のコックが同じ信州の出身だったので、言葉を交わすうちに親しくなり、厨房で炊事を手伝うこともあった。移民たちは互いに身の上話をしながら、水平線のかなたにアメリカ大陸が見える日を待った。

　楽洋丸が太平洋を越えアメリカのサンフランシスコ港に着いたのは、出港して三十日目のことである。その夜は大きな満月が、停泊中の船を照らしていた。移民として乗船していた光子たちは、それぞれ浴衣を着て甲板に上り、輪になって踊った。

　　　　　泪すは誰が子ぞ異郷の月の冴え
　　　　　　　　　　　　　　　　—あかね

その時の光子の俳句である。

the long trip to Mexico alone, she would say that, "Perhaps I was so daring because my mother died when I was very young ."

On May of 1936, Mitsuko took one last look at a field of blooming *rengesou* flowers and the melting snow on Mount Komagatake and tried to take a lasting mental picture of her hometown. Before leaving, she leans against a large nutmeg (*kaya*) tree and whispers to it, "I may never return. Please look after my family." Her beloved grandmother had said of the nutmeg that, "This tree is proof of the long and distinguished history of our family." And so, she felt the need to entrust it with her farewell and her hopes for the family she was leaving behind.

Mitsuko's older sister accompanied her as far as the Yokohama port. Because she was a picture bride, Mitsuko's name had been changed to "Mitsuko Kasuga" already, reflecting her new marital status. Of course, she was nervous about marrying a man she'd never met, but she trusted the

Rakuyoumaru
楽洋丸

matchmaker's statement that "among all his siblings, Tsutomu was who most demonstrated the virtues of filial piety." She hoped, having no choice but to go on faith, that such a man would also be kind to his future wife and children.

The belongings Mitsuko took were indicative of her values: two changes of clothing, a Japanese flag, and dozens of books. After arriving in Yokohama, Mitsuko joined two other picture brides destined for Mexico: Yone Yamazaki and Misuzu Fujisawa. The three young brides boarded the ship together and bid farewell to a Japan they were unsure they'd see again.

The ship, called Rakuyo-Maru, was a cargo vessel headed for Valparaiso, Chile. In addition to Mitsuko and the other two brides, travellers aboard were other Japanese migrants headed to South American countries, including Peru, Bolivia, Paraguay, and Argentina.

On board, Mitsuko passed the time by reading. After a few conversations with the ship's cook, who was also from Nagano, they became friendly and Mitsuko would even help him in the kitchen on occasion. The migrants talked about their lives as they waited for the day the American continent would come into view.

Thirty days after setting sail from Yokohama, the Rakuyo-Maru finished crossing the Pacific Ocean and arrived at the San Francisco Bay. Under a full moon that night, Mitsuko and her fellow travellers wore summer *kimono*s and danced in a circle on the ship's deck.

> *whose child is crying*
> *under this foreign sky*
> *with its clear and brilliant moon?*
> —Akane

The haiku Mitsuko wrote on that occasion.

Mitsuko on board (right)
船上の光子（右）

春日光子の生涯　THE LIFE OF MITSUKO KASUGA　145

3. A NEW HOME IN MEXICO

新天地メキシコ

The Rakuyo-Maru left the San Francisco Bay in June 1936, and headed for the port of Manzanillo, Mexico, where Mitsuko would disembark. At the time, Manzanillo was a small fishing village that didn't even have a pier. To disembark, passengers transferred from the Rakuyo-Maru onto a smaller boat that took them to the beach. "There are sharks everywhere," Mitsuko and the two other brides were warned as they got onto the rocking boat. Once they reached shallow waters, the boat's attendants were carried them to dry land on their backs.

On the beach, facing the ocean, was the small hut that served as an immigration office. Merchants' voices mixed with the sound of wind blowing through the coconut trees and shrill parrot calls. Among her first impressions of this new world, the sight of a dark-skinned man with a machete at his waist who pulled a donkey seared itself in her memory. As she took in the sight of large men with hairy arms and the largest eyes she had ever seen, Mitsuko couldn't help but stare. "I have come to a different world," she thought.

　1936年6月、サンフランシスコを出た楽洋丸は、目指すメキシコの港に着いた。光子が下船することになっているマンサニージョは当時、桟橋もない小さな漁師町だった。そのため、砂浜にたどりつくには楽洋丸から小舟に乗り移る必要があった。楽洋丸は沖合で一旦エンジンを止めた。光子たち三人の花嫁は揺れる小舟に乗り込み、「サメがうようよいるよ」と脅されながら岸を目指した。浅瀬に入ると、今度はむさくるしい男衆におんぶされ、ようやく陸にたどり着いたのであった。

　そこには移民の入国手続きをするための掘建て小屋だけが、海に面してぽつんと建っていた。ヤシの葉擦れの音やオウムの甲高い叫びに交じって、物売りの男の大声が光子の耳に入ってきた。山刀をさげた浅黒い肌の男がロバを引く姿が目にとまった。行き交う大男たちの腕はみな毛むくじゃらで、その目玉は見たことがないほど大きく、ギョロリと光っている。

　「私は別世界にやってきたのだ…」と、光子は実感した。

　港には、「写真花嫁」を待つ日本人移民の代表として、山崎貞男という青年が出迎えに来ていた。山崎貞男は、光子と一緒に船に乗ってきた米（よね）の結婚相手であった。のちに、光子たち夫婦とこの山崎夫妻とは、生涯にわたる親友となる。

Sadao Yamazaki, a young man who represented the Japanese husbands awaiting their brides, met the young women at the port. Yamazaki was to be Yone's husband. Over a lifetime, the Kasugas and the Yamazakis would become very close friends.

The group spent that first night in Manzanillo before boarding a train to continue their journey the next day. Their final destination was the state of San Luis Potosí, located some 600 kilometers (370 miles) inland. The train trip was overwhelming for Mitsuko, with the continuous stream of spoken Spanish serving as a constant reminder that she was now in a completely alien place.

Whenever the train passed through coconut or banana fields and stopped at a station, merchants would approach Mitsuko and speak to her loudly in Spanish. She quickly understood that they were selling the food they carried in their baskets. Once the train began moving again, the merchants would hop off, calling out *"Adios, adios!"* as they waved goodbye. Mitsuko would

---

さて、光子たち一行はマンサニージョの日本人宿に一泊したのち、汽車に乗って移動を続けた。目的地は、およそ600キロメートル離れた内陸部にあるサンルイスポトシ州である。汽車の乗客たちが大声で何やら話している様子に、光子はただ圧倒されていた。

汽車がヤシ林やバナナ畑を抜けて小さな駅に停まると、物売りたちが光子に寄って来て、大きな声で何かを言った。どうやらかごに並べた食べ物を売り歩いているようだった。光子には次第に、メキシコで出会う人々のまなざしが、どれも人懐っこいように感じられてきた。汽車が再びゆっくり動き出すと、物売りたちは「アディオス、アディオス」と言って、光子たちに手を振った。

汽車の中で知り合った永谷という日本人の男が、駅で買った茹でエビを光子たちに分けてくれた。永谷はメキシコ南部のチアパスで生活している移民で、日本から船でやって来る自分の子どもたちを出迎えにマンサニージョ港まで来ていたのだった。このときに永谷からもらったエビのおいしさは、光子にとって一生忘れられないほどだったという。

wave back to them, feeling a sense of familiarity with the people of this new country, and being comforted by their friendliness.

In addition to her introduction to the Mexican countryside, Mitsuko's train trip to San Luis Potosí also introduced her to fellow migrants. For the rest of her life, she remembered a Japanese man named Nagatani, who shared with her some boiled shrimp he'd bought at a station. Mitsuko learned that he lived in Chiapas, a state in Southern Mexico, and would fondly recall how delicious the shrimp had been.

When the train finally arrived at Cerritos, San Luis Potosí, Mitsuko stepped onto the small station platform and met Tsutomu Kasuga, the man who would be her lifelong companion, for the first time. Tsutomu and Mitsuko were 26 and 22 years old, respectively, when they met.

"Thank you for making such a long journey for me," he said shyly. Mitsuko felt the warmth behind his words and started feeling at ease with

---

　汽車はいよいよ、最終目的地であるサンルイスポトシ州・セリートスに着いた。小さな駅に下り立つと、伴侶となる春日勉が光子を迎えに来ているのが見えた。二人はそこで初めて顔を合わせた。
「遠いところへよく来てくれたね」
　とねぎらう勉の顔は、少し恥ずかしそうに見えた。光子の胸は熱くなった。
　このとき勉26歳、光子22歳であった。

　遠くに見える灰色の町が、光子がこれから暮らしてゆく場所だった。一面に広がる砂地の上に、乾ききった竜舌蘭(りゅうぜつらん)とサボテンが、土ぼこりをかぶって生えている。まわりを見渡しても緑のものは何も見当たらず、信州の青い山脈や田畑に囲まれて育った光子の目には、異様な光景に映った。
　町に着くと光子は、岩垂(いわだれ)商会に案内された。勉が住み込みで見習いとして働いている店で、これから光子もここで一緒に下働きをすることになっていた。一か月を越える長旅の末にセリートスに到着した光子であったが、特に結婚式や歓迎会が開かれるわけでもなく、翌

her decision.

Off in the distance, in the middle of an expansive desert littered with bone-dry agave and dusty cacti, sat the gray-colored town that Mitsuko would call home. There was nothing green as far as the eye could see. It was an unfamiliar sight for Mitsuko, who had grown up surrounded by the green mountains and fields of Nagano.

Once Tsutomu and Mitsuko arrived in town, he introduced her to Iwadare Commerce. This was where Tsutomu lived and worked as an apprentice, and where Mitsuko would also work. After spending a month crossing the ocean and having just arrived in Cerritos, Mitsuko started working in the shop the next day. There would be no wedding ceremony or welcome reception, just the start of her new life.

Tsutomu and Mitsuko Kasuga (right),
Sadao and Yone Yamazaki (left)
春日勉（後列右）と光子（前列右）、
山崎貞男（後列左）と米（前列左）

朝からはもう店頭に立つことが決まっていた。

4. LIFE IN CERRITOS

セリートスでの慣れない暮らし

Iwadare Commerce was a large shop in Cerritos that carried most non-food items needed for daily life. The owner, Teikichi Luis Iwadare, was also from Nagano. Mitsuko felt this job was an important first step toward settling into her new life in Mexico.

Mitsuko took the Spanish middle name Esperanza, meaning "hope," in order to appear less foreign to the Mexican people. For the same reason, Tsutomu had also taken a Spanish name, Carlos, one of the most common male names in Mexico.

In the shop, Mitsuko was instructed to ask customers, "¿Qué necesita?" (What do you need?). And while she diligently repeated the phrase, she had no idea what the Mexican customers were saying in response. Her inability to speak Spanish made working difficult, so Mitsuko made an effort to learn Spanish by listening to others. Over time, she learned product names, colors, numbers and other useful words and phrases, but it would take her some time to be able to have a meaningful conversation.

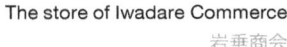
The store of Iwadare Commerce
岩垂商会

　岩垂商会はセリートスの町では大きな問屋で、生鮮食品以外ならたいていの生活雑貨を扱っていた。店を経営する岩垂貞吉は、勉や光子と同じ信州の出身であった。いよいよここがメキシコ生活のはじめの一歩になるのだと、光子は覚悟を決めた。
　メキシコ人にもなじみやすいようにと、光子には「エスペランサ」というメキシコ式のミドルネームがつけられた。「希望」という意味である。夫の勉は、メキシコで最もポピュラーな名前の一つである「カルロス」を名乗っていた。
　店に立った光子は、「ケ・ネセシータ？（何がご入り用ですか）」と言うよう指示された。仕方なくそのフレーズだけは繰り返すのだが、メキシコ人の客が返してくる言葉がさっぱりわからない。会話ができなければ仕事にならないので、光子は必死でスペイン語を聞き覚えた。そのうち少しずつ品物の名前、色の名前などを理解できるようにはなっていったが、まともに応対できるようになるまでには相当な努力が必要だった。

Life in Cerritos couldn't be more different from her life in Japan, and beyond the cultural differences, Mitsuko often struggled with the lack of conveniences. There were no lights after 10:00 p.m., so they had to live by candlelight at night. And the hardships of life in a desert climate did not end with limited electricity. In her hometown of Ina, clean fresh water had been everywhere, and households could use as much as they wanted, so it was a major shock to Mitsuko that the water she used for cooking was often mosquito-infested, and drinking water had to be purchased. They used a drum for bathing, and water had to be lifted from a well 26 meters (85 feet) deep. If she was lucky, she could bathe once per week. Mitsuko could not hide her surprise when she was asked at breakfast for the first time, "Would you like to use this water to wash your face or to make coffee?"

Despite the hardships of their lifestyle, one saving grace was that Mexican food agreed with Mitsuko. From the day she arrived in Mexico, she fell in love with foods like *tortillas*, *frijoles* (beans), and *nopales* (cactus). Filled with

Tsutomu (left) in front of a truck
岩垂商会のトラックと勉（左）

セリートスの町では、日本での生活とは勝手が違い、あまりの不便さに困惑することが多かった。午後十時になると電気が使えなくなり、ろうそくを灯して夜を過ごさなければならないし、料理をする水にはボウフラがわいていて、飲み水はお金を出して買わねばならない。ふるさと・伊那では、きれいな水がいつでも好きなだけ使えただけに、光子にはショックが大きかった。乾燥地帯の生活の厳しさはそれだけにとどまらない。入浴はドラム缶のような風呂おけで、深さ26メートルの井戸から水をくみ出して、週に一度でも体を洗えればまだましなほうだった。朝食の時間に、「水で顔を洗いますか、それともかわりにその水でコーヒーをいれましょうか」と尋ねられた時の、光子の驚きといったらなかった。

しかし、そんな慣れない生活の中でも、メキシコ料理が口に合ったのは幸いだった。メキシコに着いたその日から、トルティーヤもフリホーレス（煮豆）もウチワサボテンも、光子にはみんなおいしいと感じられた。「とにかく、この地で頑張っている夫を助けていかなく

a desire to support her husband, who was working hard to succeed in this foreign land, Mitsuko gave her best effort to adapting to life in Cerritos, and finding a love for the local food certainly made it easier for her to do so.

Mitsuko had her first child the year after arriving in Mexico. She gave birth in Iwadare Commerce's warehouse with help from the local midwife. She finally heard the cries of her first son after a long, difficult delivery. Her husband named their first child Carlos Tsuyoshi, which passed on Tsutomu's adopted name, and added the Japanese middle name Tsuyoshi to reflect their desire for their son to be strong-willed and courageous. For Mitsuko, who had grown up surrounded by sisters, the birth of a son brought immense joy.

Mitsuko and Tsutomu
光子と勉

ては…」という一心で、セリートスの生活に溶けこもうとする光子だった。

　メキシコに移住した翌年、光子は一人目の子どもを出産している。店の薄暗い倉庫に体を横たえ、村の産婆に助けられながらのお産だった。長い難産の末、男の子が産声をあげた。夫婦はこの子を「カルロス剛」と名付けた。「カルロス」は勉のメキシコ名をそのまま受け継ぐ名前で、「剛」の字には「意志の強い、剛毅な子に育つように」という願いがこめられている。女きょうだいの中で育った光子にとって、男の子の誕生はことさらうれしく心強いことであった。

Teikichi Luis Iwadare and his family
岩垂商会を経営していた岩垂貞吉と家族

Mitsuko's first baby
光子と勉に長男が誕生

Tsutomu and the first baby
長男を抱く勉

5. OPENING A STORE ON THE EVE OF WAR

Tanka 045

開戦前夜の店開き

In 1938, the year before World War II began, Tsutomu and Mitsuko decided it was time to open their own store. Japanese armed forces had invaded mainland China in 1937 and German troops would invade Poland in 1939, bringing about an age of tumultuous and dramatic change. But in Mexico, life for the Kasugas was going on without knowing that war would soon change the direction of their lives.

After eight years working at Iwadare Commerce, Tsutomu had gained the knowledge and experience to start his own business. While the birth of his son was the right incentive to open his own store, he knew he could not start the same type of business in Cerritos, when Iwadare Commerce had been good to him thus far. For this reason, Tsutomu and Mitsuko decided to move to the town of Cárdenas, still in the state of San Luis Potosí, to open their store.

Cárdenas was about 120 kilometers (75 miles) away from Cerritos and was growing as an agricultural town. It was a lively town that was home to many railroad workers. There were many Chinese and Arab immigrants living in the town, as well as four Japanese people who already owned businesses in

---

　勉と光子が独立して自分たちの店を構えることを決意したのは、第二次世界大戦が始まる前年の1938年のことである。1937年には日本軍が中国大陸に攻め入り、1939年にはドイツ軍がポーランドに侵攻するという、激動の時代でのスタートであった。

　勉はこれまで岩垂商会で働いた8年間で、起業するのに十分な知識と技能を身につけていた。子どもが生まれたのを機に独立することにしたのだが、世話になってきた岩垂商会と同じような商売をセリートスの町の中で始めるわけにはいかない。そこで二人はサンルイスポトシ州内にある、カルデナスという別の町に引っ越すことにした。

　カルデナスはセリートスから120キロメートルほどの距離にあり、農産物の集散地として発展していた。大きな駅があったため鉄道関係者も多く住み、町には活気があった。移民としては、多くの中国人やアラブ人がこの町で暮らしていたが、日本人も四人いてそれぞれに商売を手がけていた。その見知らぬ町に向かう光子の胸には、生後8か月の長男・カルロス剛がしっかりと抱かれていた。

　こうして、勉と光子はカルデナスの駅前で小さな食料雑貨店を始めた。

the town. Holding her eight-month-old son tightly, Mitsuko called upon her spirit of adventure and headed toward yet another unknown destination.

Tsutomu and Mitsuko's store opened near the train station in Cárdenas and carried everything from daily necessities and food to tools. For Japanese immigrants opening their first store, local wholesalers were extremely helpful. Additionally, Mitsuko and Tsutomu benefited from the pre-existing reputation of Japanese people being honest and hardworking. There were even farmers who trusted them simply because they were Japanese, so their business quickly grew to a size where they could purchase grain by the car. The townspeople were very welcoming of the young couple, which allowed their business to bring in a steady income.

By then, Mitsuko's Spanish had improved greatly. Aided by her fondness for chatting with people at the market, she was now able to engage in casual conversations. However, Mitsuko never stopped working to improve her language skills. In addition to learning how to speak fluently, she wanted to be able to read and write in Spanish. She practiced constantly, reviewing

---

　二人の店では、食材から金物まで生活必需品を何でもそろえていた。初めて自分の店を構えたこの日本人移民に、問屋たちは何かと便宜をはかってくれた。「日本人は正直で働き者だ」という評判を築いた、先輩移民たちのお陰である。日本人であるというだけで信用してくれる農家の人々もいて、勉たちの商売はすぐに、貨車で大量の穀類を買い付けるまでに大きくなった。夫婦の誠実な人柄もあって店はカルデナスの町の人々から歓迎され、着実に収入をあげていったのである。
　光子のスペイン語も、この頃にはずいぶん上達していた。市場などで人と言葉を交わすのが好きだったこともあり、自然な会話ができるようになっていたのである。それでも光子は、学び続ける努力を怠らなかった。会話をするだけでなく、きちんと読み書きもできなければいけない。そう考えていた光子は、スペイン語の新聞や本を手に入れては、必死にその内容を理解しようと頑張った。
　カルデナスに引っ越してから間もなく、勉と光子は二人目の子を授かった。次男・ルイス毅（たけし）である。そして、その２年後には長女・エルメリンダ美智子が生まれる。
　勉は、事業を拡大するために、町の中心部に新たに土地を買って商店を建設し始めた。そ

carefully any Spanish-language newspaper or book she came across.

Soon after moving to Cárdenas, Mitsuko became pregnant and gave birth to the couple's second child, Luis Takeshi. Two years later, she gave birth to their first daughter, Ermelinda Michiko.

Looking to expand the business, Tsutomu purchased new land in the center of town and began building a new store. This was a large-scale building that would comprise a store as well as living space and a warehouse. Both Tsutomu and Mitsuko felt rooted in Cárdenas and hoped to settle there permanently.

Unfortunately, Mitsuko's family would once again be tested by fortune. On December 7, 1941, Japan attacked the United States' navy base in Pearl Harbor. This news reached them over the radio as Mitsuko breastfed baby Ermelinda. Mitsuko immediately rushed to the store to share the news with Tsutomu.

Realizing the seriousness of this event, Tsutomu and Mitsuko felt immediate concern. Would news of Japan's attack on the United States make Mexicans see Japanese people in a different light? They could only hope that

Mitsuko with her second child
次男が誕生

れは、店に加えて住宅と倉庫も兼ねそなえた大きな建物だった。勉も光子も「カルデナスを第二のふるさととして生きてゆこう」と希望に燃えていた。

そんな一家に、時代の波が容赦なく押し寄せる。

1941年12月、日本がアメリカ合衆国の真珠湾を攻撃。そのニュースがラジオから流れたのは、光子が子どもにお乳をやっていたときだった。思わず立ち上がった光子は、店に出ていた勉に急いで知らせた。二人は不安でいっぱいになった。日本がアメリカを攻撃したというニュースのせいで、メキシコ人の日本人を見る目が変わらないだろうか。日本人排斥が起きなければよいが…。悪い考えが次々と頭をよぎる。

ニュースが町中にまわった翌朝、光子たちが恐る恐る店を開けると、一人の客が飛び込ん

there would be no widespread anti-Japanese sentiment.

By the next morning, news had spread through the town. Just as Mitsuko and Tsutomu nervously opened the store, a customer jumped towards them. To their surprise, the customer immediately embraced Tsutomu and said to Mitsuko in a happy voice, "Señora, we are winning against the U.S.!"

Instead of being viewed as enemies, they were greeted as comrades with the same pleasantness as before. Mitsuko was grateful for the warmth shown by the townsfolk.

When remembering these times, she would say that they were never treated poorly by the Mexican people due to the war. This was in large part because at that time, the general population in Mexico did not have negative feelings towards the Axis Nations (Japan, Germany, and Italy). In contrast, Mexico had a complex relationship with its northern neighbor, against whom they had lost a war, and half of its land, in the 19th century.

There's a story from that time that accurately captured the anti-American sentiment in Cárdenas. A German submarine docked at a Mexican port was

The newly constructed house
建設の終わった家

できた。驚いたことに、客は真っ先に勉に駆け寄り抱きしめたのだ。そして、明るい声で光子に言った。

「セニョーラ、僕たちはアメリカに勝っていますよ！」

敵としてではなくむしろ仲間として、変わらぬ親しさで声をかけてくれたのである。こうしたメキシコの人々の情を、光子は心からありがたいと思った。戦争を理由にメキシコ人から嫌な思いをさせられたことは、その後も一度もなかったという。

それは当時、メキシコの一般庶民の間では、日独伊の枢軸国に対して悪い感情を抱く人があまりいなかったことが関係している。メキシコは19世紀にアメリカと戦争をして敗北し、

captured by American forces and the crew was transported by train from the port in Tampico to Mexico City. Because Cárdenas was midway between these cities, the train stopped there for maintenance and to load and unload cargo. During the train's stop, the people of Cárdenas who knew of the train's passengers gathered at the station and the chant, "Hail Germany!" could be heard reverberating through town. Some townspeople gave the German prisoners fruits and folk crafts. This strong anti-American sentiment was most likely what prevented Mitsuko and Tsutomu from being seen as enemies. In fact, it was not rare for Mexicans to praise Japan and Germany saying, "Thank you for striking back at America!"

With the ongoing support of the locals, business at their store was bustling. Insufficient supply from the town's thermal power plant sometimes left them without electricity, but Mitsuko and Tsutomu never thought of leaving Cárdenas. They merely purchased a generator so they could continue doing business.

テキサスやカリフォルニアなど国土の半分を喪失した。そういった歴史的経緯などのせいで根強い反米感情があり、「よくぞアメリカをやっつけてくれた」と、日本やドイツを応援するメキシコ人も珍しくなかったという。

　カルデナスの人々の反米感情を示す、一つの話がある。戦時下のある日、メキシコ湾に潜入したドイツ潜水艦が米軍に捉えられ、乗組員たちが汽車でタンピコ港からメキシコシティに護送された。光子たちの住んでいたカルデナスはその中継点であったため、積み荷の上げ下ろしと点検のために汽車が停車した。すると、そのことを知ったカルデナスの住民が集まり、町の中心部で「ドイツ万歳！」を斉唱する声が響いたという。駅ではメキシコ人が、ドイツ人捕虜たちにさまざまな果物や民芸品を差し出す光景さえ見られた。このように心情的にアメリカに反感を抱き、枢軸国側の肩を持つ人が多かったために、光子たち日本人移民も敵視されずに済んだのだと考えられる。

　勉と光子の商店は、町の人々に支えられてますます繁盛していった。火力発電所の供給不足のため町に電気がこなくなったときでさえも、光子たちはカルデナスを去ろうとは思わず、発電機を買って商売を続けたのである。

6. FORCED MIGRATION

強制移住

Soon after the completion of the store and the house they built to expand their business, Tsutomu and Mitsuko were faced with heartbreak. As a wartime measure, the government issued a decree requiring all Japanese people living in rural Mexico to migrate to Mexico City or Guadalajara within 72 hours. At a time when they felt supported by their local community and their future was looking bright, being forced to move from Cárdenas was devastating.

Tsutomu and Mitsuko's business was based on credit (products were sold to customers with a promise of payment at a later date), but after hearing that they were being forced to leave Cárdenas, many people hurried to pay off their balances. Some people who didn't have cash sold livestock to make money in order to repay them. Mitsuko was deeply moved by the townspeople's integrity.

The day came for the Kasuga family to leave

Farewell
別れの記念写真

事業拡大のために建設した商店と家が完成した矢先、勉と光子の前に災難が舞い込む。戦時下の措置として、メキシコの地方に暮らす日本人はすべて、首都メキシコシティまたはグアダラハラに72時間以内に移住するようにという命令が出されたのである。多くのメキシコ人の好意にも支えられ「さあ、これからだ」というときに、店をたたんでカルデナスを去るのはとてもつらいことだった。

勉と光子は掛売り（代金あと払いの約束で品物を売るやり方）で食料品などの仲卸もしていたが、二人がカルデナスを去ると聞いて、多くの客が残りの代金を急いで渡そうとしてくれた。その誠実さに、光子は感激した。中には、手持ちの現金がないからと家畜の牛や豚を売ってお金を作り、支払いに駆けつけた人もいたという。

そして、光子たち夫婦がサンルイスポトシ州・カルデナスを後にする日がやってきた。6歳、4歳、2歳の三人の子どもを連れて、光子は駅で汽車を待った。発車時刻が夜中だったにもかかわらず、駅には町長、郵便局長、学校長、商売仲間など大勢の人々が詰めかけ、光子たち一家を激励した。車内で食べるようにと、手作りの軽食やお菓子を持たせてくれる人もいた。

Cárdenas, San Luis Potosí. With her three children aged 6, 4, and 2 years old, Mitsuko waited at the station for the train. Despite a nighttime departure, the town mayor, post office chief, school dean, fellow merchants, and many others came to see them off. Their support lent strength to Mitsuko's family. Some people even gave them food and snacks to eat on the train.

"Take care."

"Come back."

The people seeing them off called out to them. Normally stoic, Mitsuko could not stop the tears from rolling down her cheeks.

Unlike the Japanese people and their descendants in the United States, who were placed in internment camps during WWII, relocated Japanese people in Mexico were allowed to live normal lives in the city. However, life was still hard for Mitsuko and her family. They had been cast into a vast unknown city without a clue as to how to find work. Furthermore, the

---

「元気でな」「きっと帰ってくるんだよ」
見送りの人々が口々に声をかける。
普段決して涙を見せることのなかった光子であったが、このときばかりは、熱いものが頬を伝い落ちるのを止められなかった。

メキシコシティに集められた日本人は、強制収容所に隔離されたアメリカの日本人や日系人とは違い、町の中で生活をすることが許されていた。とはいえ、光子たちの暮らしは困難を極めた。仕事のあてもないまま、見知らぬ大都会に投げ出されたのである。さらに、戦争の情勢が毎日のように変わるため、将来の見通しを立てることもできなかった。そのような状況下で、幼い三人の子どもたちを抱えながら生活してゆくのは大変なことだった。

勉はサンルイスポトシからの友人・山崎貞男とともに、オレンジやトマトの仲卸の仕事を始めた。光子は育児と家事に追われていた。勉がやっとの思いで現金を稼いでも、インフレで物価の上昇がひどいため、家族五人分の十分な食べ物を手に入れられないこともあった。光子はメキシコシティに引っ越した翌年、流産を経験している。

status of the war changed daily, filling the future with uncertainty. Most concerning, they were trying to raise three small children in very distressing conditions.

Together with Sadao Yamazaki, the friend from San Luis Potosí who married Mitsuko's travelmate Yone, Tsutomu began working as a fruit and vegetable seller while Mitsuko devoted her energy to raising the children and taking care of the home. Despite Tsutomu's best efforts to make a living, inflation was so severe that at times they didn't have enough food to feed the family. Mitsuko suffered a miscarriage the year after they moved to Mexico City.

The Kasugas were not the only family forced into such hardship. Many Japanese immigrants in similar situations settled in various neighborhood around Mexico City. They all helped each other as they made a life for themselves. On weekends, they would get together to discuss the latest news on the war.

このような厳しい生活をしていたのは、勉と光子の一家だけではなかった。似たような境遇の日本人移民が、メキシコシティ内のいくつかの地域にまとまって居をかまえ、互いに助け合いながら暮らしていた。週末には集まって、戦況情報を交換していたという。

敵国同士となった日本とメキシコとの通信は、極度に制限されるようになっていた。光子がふるさとの家族と手紙をやりとりしたくても、届くかどうかわからず不安が募るばかり。また、やっと日本から届いた手紙にも、開封して検閲された跡が残っていて、何とも言えぬ不快な気持ちにさせられた。メキシコシティに引っ越した直後、一家はラジオもない最低限の暮らしをしていたので、日本の情勢が皆目わからない。メキシコの日系移民コミュニティーでは、「神国日本」の華々しい戦果を信じて疑わない人が大勢を占めていたが、確固とした証拠があるわけではなかった。日々混乱が深まる状況の中で、遠く信州・伊那に暮らす父や姉妹のことが心配でたまらない光子であった。

ある日、勉が小さなラジオを手に入れてきた。勉と光子は毎晩こっそりと日本の大本営発表を受信し始めた。スペイン語のニュースを聞き取ることのできた二人は、密かに聞く日本の大本営発表と、アメリカ側を主な情報源とするスペイン語ニュースの間に極端な違いがあ

Since Japan and Mexico had become enemy nations during of the war, communication between the countries was restricted to the bare minimum. Even though Mitsuko tried to exchange letters with her family in Japan, there was no guarantee that letters reached them. And letters that did arrive from Japan were often open, which felt like a violation.

Immediately after moving to Mexico City, the family's situation was so dire that they didn't even have a radio, so they had no idea about the situation in Japan. Among the community of Japanese immigrants in Mexico, most held an unwavering belief that the divine nation of Japan would achieve a staggering victory, but they had nothing beyond faith to back up this conviction. Faced with living conditions that grew ever more turbulent, Mitsuko constantly worried for her father and sisters in her faraway homeland.

One day, Tsutomu managed to obtain a small radio to help alleviate the stress caused by the lack of news on the war. Every night, Tsutomu and

---

ることに気がついた。日本が総崩れの状況になっているであろうことを把握した勉と光子であったが、その実情を他の日本人移民に流布すれば国賊として糾弾される恐れがあるため、ごく限られた人に知らせるにとどめたのであった。

Mitsuko would listen quietly to the announcements from Japan's Imperial Headquarters. The couple began noticing significant differences between the official Japanese news programs and the Mexican counterpart, which was based on U.S. sources. Tsutomu and Mitsuko realized that Japan was on the verge of losing the war. However, they worried that they would be treated as traitors to their homeland if they shared this information with other Japanese immigrants, so they only discussed this information with a small, trusted group.

Mexico City (1940-1950)
1940–50 年頃のメキシコシティ

7. STARTING OVER AFTER THE WAR

戦後の新規まき直し

Mitsuko was 31 years old when the war ended on August 1945. This meant that it was time for Tsutomu and Mitsuko to fully embrace the challenge of starting over.

First of all, thinking of the children's education made the family stay in Mexico City, which had many good schools. Tsutomu returned to San Luis Potosí, where they still had a store and a home full of memories, to sell their property.

It was also around this time that Mitsuko and Tsutomu went through the bittersweet milestone of obtaining their Mexican citizenship. Although this represented their commitment to plant roots in Mexico and build a life there, it also meant giving up their Japanese citizenship. However, Mexican citizenship would make it easier for them to purchase property and run a business. Mitsuko was also happy that, as a Mexican citizen, she would have the right to vote.

To further embrace her new life, Mitsuko was baptized into the Catholic

---

1945年8月の終戦を迎えたとき、光子は31歳になっていた。この年、勉と光子は子育てから事業に至るまで、新規まき直しの挑戦を始める。

二人はまず、子どもたちの教育のことを考え、良い学校が数多くあるメキシコシティでこのまま暮らし続けることを決断した。サンルイスポトシ州・カルデナスに残してきた思い出の商店と家は、勉が現地に行って売却した。

光子と勉がメキシコ国籍を取得したのもこの時期であった。それは、メキシコに根を張り生きていこうという二人の決意の表れであったが、同時に、日本国籍を手放すということも意味していた。しかし、メキシコ人になれば、不動産の購入やビジネスの立ち上げがしやすくなるというメリットがある。メキシコの国民として選挙権が得られるのも、光子にはうれしかった。

さらに、光子はキリスト教の洗礼も受けている。これは、国民の大多数がカトリック教徒であるメキシコの社会に溶け込むための努力であるとともに、自分の子どもたちが社会で不利益を受けないようにとの配慮でもあった。

church. Not only was this part of her effort to blend into a Mexican society, where the vast majority of people are Roman Catholic, but it also helped ensure that their children would not face unnecessary hardships in Mexican society.

The end of the war made it possible for the family to start working on a long-term plan to support itself. Tsutomu and Sadao Yamazaki stopped working as fruit and vegetable sellers and opened up a confectionary called *Dulcería San Juan*. In addition to confections, fruit, and other foodstuff, the shop carried gift items and other sundries.

Tsutomu and Sadao lived only two blocks from each other, so the two families were able to help each other as needed. The two wives had grown so close that each week Mitsuko and Yone would split up the task of preparing lunch for Tsutomu and Sadao.

Tsutomu and Sadao even purchased a car together

Mitsuko and Yone
光子（右）と米

戦争が終わったことによって長期的な見通しを立てられるようになったので、春日勉と山崎貞男はオレンジやトマトの仲卸をやめ、共同で菓子屋（Dulcería San Juan）を始めた。菓子や果物などの食品の他、贈答品や生活雑貨なども扱う小売店である。

春日家のアパートと山崎家のアパートは2ブロックしか離れていなかったので、両家はいつも助け合いながら生活をしていた。それは、山崎貞男の妻・米と光子が、同じ船でメキシコに渡ってきた仲間だったからこそできたことで、例えば勉と貞男が店で食べるための弁当作りは、光子と米が週ごとに分担を決め、二人分をまとめて作るようにしていた。

自動車は両家共同で購入し、交代で乗っては商売や生活に利用していた。また、山崎家にも子どもが三人いたので、両家の子どもたちのためにお金を出し合って、スペイン語の百科事典『若人の宝』を買い、20冊セットのものを10冊ずつ両家で分けた。子どもたちはときどき本を交換しながら、夢中で読みふけった。

時代が大きく動いた終戦の年が暮れようとする頃、チャプルテペック病院で次女・マルタ悠紀子が生まれた。光子にとって四人目の子どもであったが、設備の整った病院で出産した

and took turns driving for work and using it for other family needs. And because the Yamazakis also had three children, both families pitched in to purchase The "Treasure of Youth," a Spanish-language encyclopedia set. Each family kept ten volumes of the twenty-volume set in their home. The children would periodically exchange the books and often read them together.

The year 1945 would still hold more changes for the Kasugas. Mitsuko's second daughter, Marta Yukiko, was born toward the end of the year at Chapultepec Hospital. Though it was Mitsuko's fourth birth, this was the first time she'd ever given birth in a hospital with proper facilities and equipment.

Hoping to comfort Mitsuko after a difficult birth, Tsutomu brought her Welch's Grape Juice. This drink was an American brand-name product that was a luxury purchase for a struggling

Tsutomu and Mitsuko
勉と光子

のはこれが初めてある。
　難産で弱っている光子を見舞うために、勉がウェルチのぶどうジュースを持ってきた。苦しい家計の中からお金を出して買った、米国ブランドの特別な飲み物である。光子はベッドの上でジュースを口に含み、満足そうな顔をした。
　「お産の間が私の休暇だった。ベッドの上に寝転んで、ゆっくりできるんだからね」と、のちに光子は振り返っている。

　春日勉と山崎貞男が始めた菓子屋には、順調に客がついた。
　店のオープンから1年余りが経った1947年、勉はこの店の経営を山崎貞男に任せて、自分は別の菓子屋を開くことにした。子どもが増えるにつれて、一つの店舗の収入で二家族を養うことが難しくなってきたからだ。勉と貞男は仕事の面では分かれることになったが、その後も生涯にわたって大親友であり続ける。

　勉が新たに始めた店（Dulcería Uruguay）も、ほどなくして軌道に乗った。この菓子屋

family. Mitsuko sat in her hospital bed enjoying the taste of the delicious juice.

"Childbirth was my vacation. It was the only time I could lay in bed and take it easy," Mitsuko would recall.

Tsutomu and Sadao's shop gradually became more popular with customers. They were successful enough that in 1947, about a year after opening the first shop, Tsutomu decided to entrust Sadao with the management of the store so he could open another confectionary. As their families grew, it was becoming difficult for one shop to support both families' needs. Although Tsutomu and Sadao split the business, their friendship remained strong throughout their lifetime.

Tsutomu's new shop,

Tsutomu's new store
勉が開いた菓子屋

の前には、近郊から通勤する人たちが乗り降りするバス停があって、店には客足が絶えなかった。勉は筋金入りの働き者であったが、それに加えて商売のセンスもあったようである。

朝の10時から閉店の10時まで、勉はずっと自分の店に立ち続けた。法で定められた休日（元日とメキシコ独立記念日の二日間）以外は土日も休まず店を開け、子どもたちが起きているうちに帰宅できることはまずなかった。しかし、閉店後は必ず子どもの人数分だけお菓子の包みを作って家に持ち帰る、子煩悩な父親でもあった。子どもたちは、朝起きてその包みを開けるのを楽しみにしていた。子どもたちの笑顔を見ることが、勉の何よりの生き甲斐だった。

菓子屋の経営のかたわら、勉はアンズの加工品を作る仕事も始めた。事業立ち上げのヒントになったのは、光子の愚痴である。一家は4階建てのアパートに住んでいたが、光子が梅干しを作るため塩漬けした梅を屋上に干しておくと、同じアパートに住むメキシコ人の子どもたちがこっそり食べてしまうという出来事が何度か続いた。光子は嘆いたが、それを聞いた勉は、「これはメキシコで商売になるぞ」と思いついたのだ。何事にも楽観的で、前向きな勉ならではの目のつけどころであったと言える。

Dulcería Uruguay, was up and running quickly. Tsutomu was a hard worker but he also had a keen sense for business, which was reflected in his choice of location. In front of the new shop there was a bus stop used by people coming to work from outlying areas. The shop soon had an endless stream of customers.

Tsutomu worked in his shop from 10 a.m. to closing at 10 p.m. Other than the two legally mandated holidays (New Year and Independence Day), Tsutomu never took days off and even worked Saturdays and Sundays. He never made it back home while his children were awake. However, after he closed the shop for the day, Tsutomu always took treats home for his children. Tsutomu was an affectionate father. Every day his children looked forward to waking up and eating the treats Tsutomu had brought them. And for Tsutomu, seeing the smiling faces of his children in the morning was a source of joy.

As an extension of running a confectionary, Tsutomu began to

梅干しにヒントを得て開発した勉の干しアンズは、その後メキシコでヒット商品となった。かつてセリートスで勉を育てた岩垂貞吉も、同時期に干しアンズの商品を独自に開発。液体や粉にした岩垂貞吉の商品は売れに売れ、メキシコの他の食品メーカーがこぞって同じようなものの製造・販売を始めたほどだった。この干しアンズは中国の干し梅から名前をとって「チャモイ」と呼ばれ、今ではメキシコ人なら誰もが知る定番の味となっている。

manufacture sun-dried apricots. The idea for this business came from a complaint Mitsuko made. At that time, the family lived in a 4-story apartment building and whenever Mitsuko would place her homemade pickled apricots on the rooftop to dry, the building's children would sneak up and eat them. Ever the optimist and creative person, it occurred to Tsutomu that there may be a market in México for these Japanese-style dried fruits.

Tsutomu's dried apricots eventually became a nationwide hit in Mexico. Today, this treat, named *chamoy* after the Chinese word for dried plums, is a staple of Mexican food culture. In fact, Teikichi Luis Iwadare, for whom Tsutomu had apprenticed at Iwadare Commerce, was developing his own version of *chamoy* around the same time. Iwadare developed liquified and pulverized versions of *chamoy*, which continued to grow in popularity. Eventually, other Mexican food manufacturers also started to produce and sell them. Thus *chamoy* has now become a classic flavor that makes Mexicans' mouth water.

Tsutomu in front of the refrigerator. He always had enterprise to try new products like fruites from California, cheese, ham and beverages.
冷蔵庫の前に立つ勉。新しい物を取り入れることに積極的だった勉は、アメリカのカリフォルニアからぶどうや桃を輸入していたほか、ハム、チーズ、飲料などの販売も手がけていた。

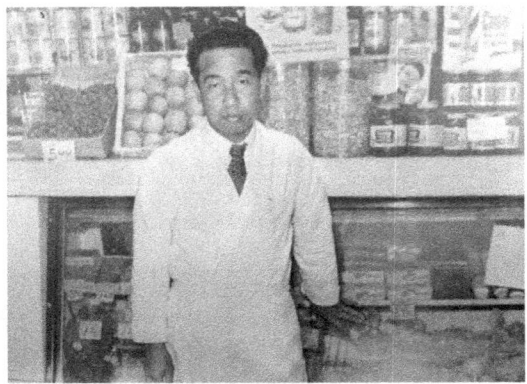

8. RAISING SIX CHILDREN

Tanka 003–006, 014, 046, 047, 054

六人の子育て

Between 1947 and 1948, Mitsuko gave birth to two more girls (Esperanza Masako and María Teresa Miwako), bringing them to a total of six children squeezed into a small, two-bedroom apartment.

Mitsuko's daily routine was a hectic mix of helping Tsutomu with work and taking care of the children. To feed six growing children, Mitsuko conceived of a dish she called the "Hungry Kids' Stew." To be able to feed the kids immediately at any time, Mitsuko kept a large pot simmering with a mix of beef and vegetables spiced with *miso* paste. Mitsuko boasted that this dish helped her children grow big and strong.

There were eleven years between the oldest of the Kasuga children, Carlos Tsuyoshi, and the youngest, María Teresa Miwako. Squabbling between six siblings so close in age was a constant thing, but they always supported each other. For instance, their daughter Marta Yukiko was a sickly child and it was her older brother who took her to the hospital every time she needed to go.

　1947年から48年にかけて、光子はさらに二人の女の子（エスペランサ真佐子、マリアテレサ美和子）に恵まれた。子どもは合わせて六人になった。寝室が二つしかないアパートの中に、家族八人がひしめき合っていた。

　光子の毎日は、勉の仕事を助けながらの家事と育児で多忙を極めた。そこで光子は、食欲旺盛な六人の子どもたちのために、自ら名付けた「子育て鍋」なる料理を考えた。子どもたちにいつでもすぐに食べさせるように、牛肉や野菜などを大きな鍋に入れて作った味噌鍋である。これのおかげで子どもたちがすくすく大きくなっているのだと、光子は胸を張った。

　一番上のカルロス剛と、末っ子のマリアテレサ美和子との年の差は11年。互いに年の近い六人のきょうだいは、日々けんかをしながらも助け合って育っていった。たとえば、病気がちだった次女のマルタ悠紀子を一日おきに病院に連れて行くのは、兄の役割。両親と兄二人がそろって働きに出かけて家が留守になるとき、幼い三人の妹たちに夕食を食べさせて寝かしつけるのは、長女のエルメリンダ美智子の役割だった。

When both parents and the two older brothers went out to work, the oldest daughter, Ermelinda Michiko, fed her three younger sisters and put them to bed.

Believing it would offer great learning opportunities, Mitsuko and Tsutomu often had their children help out at the store.

"I want them to learn from a young age the difficulty and joy of earning a living. This experience will be useful when they become adults and have to stand on their own," Mitsuko would say.

Wrapping the snacks they sold was a perfect task for the children. You could sometimes hear the younger children complain, "My fingers hurt,"

With six children
六人の子どもたちと

　光子と勉は、教育的な観点から子どもたちによく店の手伝いをさせた。「働いてお金を稼ぐことの大変さとおもしろさを、子どものうちから学ばせたい。その経験は、やがて子どもたちが成人し社会に出るときにきっと役に立つ」と考えてのことである。店で売る菓子を包む作業は、子どもたちに労働を体験させるいい機会であった。幼い子らは、「もう指が痛くなった」とこぼしながらも両親を手伝った。「今夜はキャラメルを250グラム包もう」「明日はドライフルーツを25キロ分ラッピングしてしまおう」と目標を立てる。すると不思議と頑張れる。そんなことを子どもたちは自然に学んでいった。店の一部の棚の陳列を、子どもたちに任せることもあった。六人の子らは自分が担当する棚の売り上げが伸びるよう、競い合うようにして工夫をこらした。

　年に数度の、店が休みの日は、子どもたちを車に乗せて近郊にピクニックに連れ出した。たとえ一時（いっとき）であっても、苦しい生活のことを忘れて楽しむ野外料理の味は格別であった。普段は子どもたちに厳しい光子も、こういうときは思い切り楽しみ、朗らかに笑った。

but they still worked hard to help their parents. Setting goals like, "Let's wrap 250 grams (half pound) of caramels tonight," and "Tomorrow we'll wrap 25 kilos (55 pounds) of dried fruit," worked to encourage them. In this hardworking and busy environment, the children learned naturally. Eventually, Mitsuko and Tsutomu put the children in charge of stocking some of the store's shelves. The children would compete against one another to come up with ideas that would increase sales for their respective shelves.

The few times a year when the store was closed, the Kasugas would pile into the car and go out to the suburbs for a picnic. Even if for only a short time, the feel of the outdoors and the taste of picnic food helped them forget about their struggles. Even Mitsuko, who was normally quite strict with her children, enjoyed those moments and would smile and laugh wholeheartedly.

---

9. A TIME FOR EDUCATION

Tanka 007, 009, 012, 013, 015, 016, 029, 030, 037

暮らしの安定と教育への熱意

One day in 1949, Tsutomu purchased a refrigerator. The entire family was excited to have such a fancy appliance, and would marvel that their refrigerator even made ice. However, for Mitsuko, who was accustomed to going to the market every day to purchase fresh ingredients, it was difficult to change her routine after the arrival of their refrigerator.

The next item introduced into Mitsuko's home after the fancy refrigerator was a washing machine, followed by a vacuum cleaner and a blender. These home appliances were still rare sights at the time, but Tsutomu believed in investing in things that would help Mitsuko run the household more easily. It also gave Mitsuko great pleasure to see her children's excited faces when they came back from school to find fresh melon juice made with their blender.

Mitsuko n the kitchen
台所に立つ光子

勉が冷蔵庫を買ってきたのは、1949年のある日のことである。氷を作ることもできる最新の機械に、家族はみんな興奮した。ただ、毎日市場に行って、その日のうちに調理するという光子の習慣は、冷蔵庫が来てからもなかなか変わらなかったという。

冷蔵庫に続いて家に導入されたのは、洗濯機だった。ついで掃除機、ミキサーがやってきた。いずれも当時はまだ珍しい家電製品だったが、勉には進取の精神というものがあったようである。特に光子の家事の助けになる場合には、その精神が大いに発揮された。学校から帰ってきた子どもたちが、ミキサーで作ったメロンジュースを見つけて歓声をあげるのを見て、光子の心は喜びで満たされるのであった。

1952年、一家は念願の一軒家に引っ越しをする。コロニアル様式のその家には、寝室が三部屋と浴室が二つあり、応接間、居間、台所、食堂、さらには地下室を備えていた。子どもたちは、庭付きのこの新しい家に大はしゃぎだった。

翌53年、勉は二軒目の菓子屋（Dulcería La Esperanza）を開いた。一軒目の菓子屋

In 1952, the family was finally able to fulfilled their dream of moving into a single-family home. The colonial-style home had three bedrooms and two bathrooms as well as a parlor, living room, kitchen, dining room, and basement. The children loved their new house and its garden.

The following year, Tsutomu opened his second store, *Dulcería La Esperanza*. It was six years after the opening of his first confectionary, *Dulcería Uruguay*, and business was doing well. The new shop was close to a newspaper building, a convenient location with a lot of foot traffic. Tsutomu invited a friend and his family living in San Luis Potosí to move to Mexico City to help him run the second store.

Tsutomu had a very compelling reason to work hard to expand the business: his children's education expenses were increasing every year. Tsutomu and Mitsuko had decided to spare nothing when it came to their

El Colegio Alemán
ドイツ系の学校で学ぶ末娘

(Dulcería Uruguay) のオープンから６年がたち、商いは順調に大きくなっていた。新しい店舗は新聞社のビルに近く、人通りが多い好立地にあった。勉は、サンルイスポトシに住んでいた友人一家をメキシコシティに呼び寄せ、ともにこの店の経営を行った。

勉には、積極的にビジネスを広げる理由があった。年々ふくらむ、子どもの学費である。子どもの教育には妥協しないと決めていた勉と光子は、六人きょうだいのうちの四人をドイツ系の学校へ、残る二人はキリスト教系の女子校へ通わせていた。どちらもメキシコシティ指折りの私立名門校である。特にドイツ系の学校は、学費が市内で一番高いことでも知られていた。

さらに夫婦には、将来は子どもたちを大学に進ませたい、できれば海外にも留学させたいという希望があった。それは、当時の一家の収入レベルからすると、途方もない夢に思えた。しかし、あきらめるわけにはいかない。勉は、ビジョン実現のためにさまざまなアイデアを練り、それをすぐ実行に移していくという類まれな行動力の持ち主だった。二軒目の菓子屋開店は、勉の理想を実現するための大切な一歩であったと言える。

children's education, and were sending four of them to a German school and the other two to a Catholic girls' school. The German school, in particular, was famous for being the most expensive school in Mexico City.

The couple also hoped to send their kids to college and, if possible, send them to study abroad. Of course, studying overseas was a distant dream considering the family's resources at the time, but they were determined to do whatever they could to see this come true. Tsutomu had many ideas for achieving this vision and was the type to immediately act on them. Opening the second confectionary was an important step towards being able to fulfilling his goals.

Mitsuko was not as strong with numbers as Tsutomu, so she left the family's financial matters as well as management of the store in her husband's hands. Mitsuko focused her efforts on running the family's daily life and supporting Tsutomu's business plans. Together, Tsutomu and Mitsuko

Moved to a single-family house
一軒家に引っ越し

一方光子は、勉のようにビジネス・センスがあるわけではなかった。そこで、家計の長期プランや店の経営についてはすべて勉に任せ、自らは計画遂行のための裏方に徹した。勉と光子は、二人三脚でがむしゃらに頑張った。

子どもたち日本語は、放課後に光子自身が先生となって教えこんだ。三女のエスペランサ真佐子や末娘のマリアテレサ美和子には、日本舞踊や茶道も習わせた。メキシコで生まれ育った子どもに、日本の文化や言葉を伝えていくというのは、並大抵の決意ではできないことである。漢字の練習をいやがる幼い娘のそばに光子が座り、ついには母娘ともども泣き出してしまったことも一度ならずあったという。

光子の教育への熱意は強く、のちに自宅を開放して、日系の子どものための日本語塾を作ったほどだった。応接間、居間、食堂を改装して机を置いたスペースが教室となった。授業時間は通常の学校の放課後である午後2時半から始まり、午後5時まで。二十人から三十人の子どもたちが、低学年と高学年のクラスに分かれて日本語の学習に取り組んだ。光子も低

worked tirelessly to ensure their family's wellbeing.

An important element of the children's education was to learn about their heritage, so Mitsuko taught the children Japanese after school. Her third daughter, Esperanza Masako, and youngest daughter, María Teresa Miwako, also had lessons in Japanese dance and tea ceremony. Teaching Mexico-born Japanese children about their culture and language was not a small commitment. More than once, when Mitsuko sat with one of her young children, who hated studying kanji characters, the lesson would conclude with both mother and child bursting into frustrated tears.

The school in Mitsuko's house
自宅に開設した日本語塾

学年クラスの先生として教壇に立ったが、授業中は厳しかったという。しかし、時には庭で学芸会や運動会なども開催し、日本語塾は子どもたちにとって楽しい集いの場ともなっていた。

　光子は普段、人前に出るときはおしとやかだったが、家では口うるさい母親の顔を持っていた。特に、子どものご飯の食べ方やあいさつの仕方には厳しく、本気で腹を立てると大声で怒鳴るだけでは済まず、子どもを叩いたり物を投げつけたりすることもあったという。
　幼い頃からの光子の負けず嫌いは、六人の子の母親となっても変わらなかった。いや、むしろさらに競争意識が強くなったふしがある。自分の子の成績が学校でトップでないと知ると、光子はたちまち不機嫌になった。子どもたちの弱音や言い訳には、一切耳を貸さない。そんな母親を恐れた子どもたちは、点数の悪いテストは親に見られないよう、すぐ捨ててしまうようになった。
　光子は自分自身が長年我慢と努力を重ねて生きてきただけに、子どもたちにも同じことを求める傾向があった。目標に届かないときは、もっと努力をすればいい。これが光子の信念である。こうした厳格な母親である光子に対し、反発する子もいれば、逆にその期待に応え

Mitsuko was so passionate about education that she eventually opened a Japanese language school in the family home. They renovated the parlor, living room, and dining room to create space for a classroom with desks. Class started at 2:30 p.m., after children finished with regular school, and ended at 5:00 p.m. Twenty to thirty children were divided into junior and senior classes for Japanese study. Mitsuko taught the junior class and was known for being very strict during class. However, she would also hold arts and athletic festivals in the garden, making the Japanese language school a fun place for the children.

Mitsuko supervising the recital of the school
自宅庭で開く学芸会を見守る光子

ようと背伸びをする子もいた。
　こうした高圧的に要求を押しつける子育ては、現代においては模範的なスタイルと言えないかもしれない。しかし、一つ確かなのは、真剣に生きる母の姿を通して、子どもたちは人生の知恵を自ら学びとっていったということである。
　勉は朝から晩まで仕事に打ち込んでいたので、家にいる時間が短かった。そのため光子は、勉の分まで子どもの叱り役にまわらなければならなかった。料理や洗濯、掃除などの家事を一人でこなすかたわら、六人の子どものけんかを仲裁したり、宿題をみたり、寝かしつけたりするのである。子ども一人ひとりの話にじっくり耳を傾けたいと思っても、とてもそんな余裕はなかったであろう。
　一方、勉は休みの日になると、子どもたちを連れ出しては一緒に遊んだり、おもしろい話を聞かせてやったりした。「なるようになる」が口癖の、楽観的で寛大な父親であった。春日一家としては、のびのびと子育てをする勉と、厳しくしつけようとする光子とでうまくバランスがとれていたようである。

Outside the home, Mitsuko was seen as a very ladylike, controlled person, but at home she was free to express her displeasure when needed. She was particularly strict about her children's table manners and how they greeted people. When she was really upset, not only would she yell at her children, she would use physical punishment, and would even throw things if provoked enough.

Mitsuko believed that when you failed to reach a goal, you just needed to work harder. Furthermore, she had always hated losing, and this aspect of her personality did not change after she became a mother. In fact, her competitive side only grew stronger with age. After many years enduring hardship and working very hard just to get by, Mitsuko expect the same fortitude from her children. She would get annoyed if her children didn't have the best grades in their class and she never accepted excuses. Fearing their mother's disappointment, the children would throw away tests on which they scored poorly. Some of the children rebelled against Mitsuko's demands,

Their daughter, María Teresa Miwako, Performing classical Japanese dance
日本舞踊を披露する末娘・マリアテレサ美和子

while others worked very hard to meet her expectations.

Mitsuko's educational philosophy might not be considered the ideal style by modern standards, but her example of hard work and complete devotion to her family became a guiding light for her children.

Tsutomu worked most days from early morning to late at night, so his time at home was very limited. This left Mitsuko with the responsibility of being the disciplining hand in addition to doing the cooking, washing, cleaning, and other housework by herself. She also had to arbitrate fights between six siblings, check their homework, and put them to bed. So many demands on her time and energy meant that it was impossible for Mitsuko to spend time listening to each child's every concern.

On the occasions when Tsutomu did have a day off, he would take the children out to play and tell them stories. He was an optimistic father who would often say, "Whatever will happen, will happen." Tsutomu's sunny personality and Mitsuko's strict style provided balance for the family.

Mitsuko was very strict both as a mother and as a teacher
光子は、母としても教師としても厳しかった

Tsutomu reading at home
自宅で読書する勉

10. TANKA AND THE CACTUS

Tanka 032–036, 038–040, 049

短歌とサボテン

Mitsuko began to devote herself seriously to writing tanka and haiku around the age of 40. This was when Mitsuko chose the pen name Akane. Mitsuko had completely embraced life in Mexico, but she still had strong feelings for her homeland. She chose her pen name in honor of the auburn tinge of Ina's evening sky.

In 1955, the Japanese Ambassador to Mexico promoted the launch of poetry societies for Japanese people and their descendants living in Mexico City. Mitsuko was among the first to joins.

Having friends with whom to enjoy Japanese poetry further encouraged Mitsuko's writing. Until that point, Mitsuko had occasionally written both

Founding members of
Tanka & Haiku Club
「句歌の集い」創設メンバー

　光子が本格的に短歌と俳句に取り組み始めたのは、40歳を迎えた頃であった。1955年、当時の在メキシコ日本大使の呼びかけにより、メキシコシティに暮らす日本人・日系人を中心とした「句歌の集い」が発会し、光子はその創設メンバーになったのである。
　このとき光子は、自分の雅号を「あかね」に決めた。メキシコの生活にすっかり溶け込んだ光子であったが、一方で望郷の念も強かった。ふるさと伊那の、あの茜色に染まった夕景の象徴として、「あかね」を選んだのである。
　日本語の詩歌を楽しむ仲間の存在は、光子が詩作を行ううえで大きな励みとなった。それまでも折にふれ短歌や俳句を書き留めてきた光子だが、作品を発表したり批評し合ったりするのは初めてである。仲間に支えられ、光子は毎日のように詩作を楽しむようになった。暮らしの中で感じる喜びや悲しみや怒り。どんな思いも歌に託して表現すると、不思議と心が安らぐのだった。
　光子にとって短歌は、自らを解き放つ場であったと言えるだろう。短歌の中でなら、「母」や「妻」という役割から離れて、一人の人間として世界と向き合うことができた。

tanka and haiku, but this was the first time that she shared her work and opened herself to outside criticism. Encouraged by friends, Mitsuko soon began to write on a daily basis. Pouring the joy, sadness, or anger she felt during her day into words brought her an unexpected peace of mind.

To Mitsuko, tanka provided a space in which she could be completely free. In her tanka, she was neither "mother" nor "wife." In poetry, Mitsuko found a way to engage with the world as an individual.

At the same time that Mitsuko was embracing an identity as a poet, she was also participating in the Mexico *Shaboten Kai* (Cactus Society). The

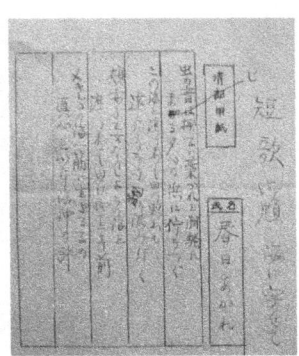

Mitsuko's handwritten tanka
光子が書いた習作

　光子がメキシコ・シャボテン会に参加していたのもこの時期である。メキシコ・シャボテン会とは、メキシコの植物について研究する学者や愛好家の集まりで、メキシコ国立自治大学の植物学者であった日系移民の松田英二博士が、中心メンバーとなっていた。松田英二はキリスト教思想家・内村鑑三の弟子で、メキシコ全土で750余りの新種植物を発見したうえ、60万点にものぼる植物標本を作り、「メキシコ植物学の父」と呼ばれている人物である。このシャボテン会の月例会は、しばしば光子の家で開かれた。メキシコ人の研究者たちは光子の手料理を楽しみにしていて、春日邸が会場になる月はいつもより参加人数が多くなるほどだった。

　光子はサボテンが大好きだった。その大きさや形の多様さも魅力的だったが、何よりもとげの中から顔を出す鮮やかな花の可憐さに強く惹き付けられた。生命力の強いサボテンに、メキシコで生きる自らの姿を重ね合わせていたのかもしれない。やる気と教養あふれるシャボテン会の仲間に囲まれ、光子は大いに刺激を受けた。時折企画されるシャボテン会の調査旅行に参加するのはもちろんのこと、週末に家族だけで出かけるピクニックでも、その土地のサボテンを探しては観察する熱心さだった。

Mexico *Shaboten Kai* was a group of academics and enthusiasts researching Mexican flora. One of the core members was Dr. Eizi Matsuda, a Japanese botanist who worked at the *Universidad Nacional Autónoma de México* (UNAM). Dr. Matsuda had discovered over 750 species of new plants throughout Mexico and had created a herbarium cataloging 600,000 plants. Dr. Matsuda was considered the father of botany in Mexico. The *Shaboten Kai*'s monthly meetings were often held at the Kasuga's home, where the Mexican researchers looked forward to Mitsuko's home cooking, resulting in larger-than-normal turnouts.

Mitsuko loved cacti. She was attracted to the diversity of their size and

Eizi Matsuda and the newsletters of *Shaboten Kai*
松田英二とメキシコ・シャボテン会の会報

サボテン好きが高じた光子は、やがて自宅の庭にも小さなサボテン園を作りあげた。庭で自転車に乗って遊んでいた末娘がサボテンの上に倒れこんでしまったとき、光子は娘のけがよりも、サボテンが無事かどうかをまず気にかけたというエピソードが残っている。

shape, but was particularly enthralled by the brilliant flowers that bloomed among the sharp thorns. Perhaps Mitsuko saw herself in the cactus—strong and vital despite its severe environment. In the *Shaboten Kai*, Mitsuko was surrounded by friends who exuded intellectual curiosity and refinement. The group was a great source of inspiration for her. In addition to joining the occasional *Shaboten Kai* research trip, Mitsuko also spent time observing local cacti whenever her family would go on trips.

Mitsuko eventually decided to create a small cactus patch in her family garden where she could nurture these plants she was coming to love so dearly. In fact, she was so devoted to these plants that when her youngest daughter fell on a cactus while riding her bike, Mitsuko was more distressed about the condition of her cactus than she was about her daughter's scratches.

Mitsuko and Tsutomu having a picnic
ピクニックを楽しむ光子と勉

11. A FAMILY REUNION

Tanka 048

父との再会

The year 1955 brought particularly good news for Mitsuko. Her father, Inao Osaka, who still lived in Japan, would travel to Mexico for the first time to meet Mitsuko's family. Inao, who had survived the horrors of the war in Japan, was 72 years old. Tsutomu had arranged for an airline ticket so that Mitsuko and her father could see each other.

It was the first time father and daughter saw each other in nearly 20 years. Mitsuko and Inao talked endlessly, as if hoping to fill the void caused by twenty years of absence. For the first time in as many years, Mitsuko was able to be a daughter again and allow her heart to feel nostalgia for her hometown.

When it came time for Inao to return to Japan, Carlos Tsuyoshi, Mitsuko's oldest son, left with him. Tsutomu had wanted his son, who was born and raised in Mexico, to see Japan

Mitsuko welcoming her father at the airport
父・伊那雄が空港に到着

1955年、光子にはうれしいことがあった。日本で暮らす父・小坂伊那雄が、光子たち一家に会うために初めてメキシコシティへ来ることになったのだ。

日本で厳しい戦争時代を生き抜いた伊那雄は、もう72歳になっていた。少しでも早く光子と伊那雄が再会できるように、勉が伊那雄の飛行機チケットを手配したのだった。

ほぼ20年ぶりの親子の対面である。空白の年月を埋めようとするかのように、光子と伊那雄は語り続けた。光子は久々に娘に返り、頭の中にはふるさとの光景がどこまでも広がっていった。

伊那雄が日本に帰るとき、一緒に付き添って行ったのは光子の長男・カルロス剛だった。メキシコで生まれ育った息子に、一度日本を見せてやりたいと考えていた勉の計らいである。勉と光子自身は移住後まだ一度も里帰りしたことがなく、望郷の念は強かったが、若い息子の留学を優先させたのである。このときカルロス剛は、好奇心旺盛な18歳の青年に成長していた。

祖父の伊那雄とともに船で太平洋を越えたカルロス剛は、親類のところに身を寄せて日本

at least once. Although neither Tsutomu nor Mitsuko had returned home since migrating to Mexico and they both had a strong desire to return, they decided to give the opportunity instead to their son. At the time, Carlos was a 18-year-old man full of youthful energy and curiosity.

After crossing the Pacific Ocean with his grandfather, Carlos Tsuyoshi stayed with relatives to learn more about Japanese language and culture before going on to study at Sophia University and at the Tokyo YMCA. Working part time at a company in Tokyo called Seidensha Industries, he learned plastic processing skills. The skills Carlos Tsuyoshi learned during his time in Japan would eventually prove beneficial to the expansion of the family business in Mexico.

New Year's Day with Inao Osaka
メキシコで一家
そろって迎えた新年

語や日本文化を吸収したのち、上智大学や東京ＹＭＣＡで学んだ。さらに、東京の精電舎工業という会社でアルバイトをしながら、ビニールを加工する技術を身につけた。ちなみに精電舎工業とは、のちに日本で熱狂的なブームを呼んだ「ダッコちゃん」人形の製造機メーカーとして有名になった会社である。このときにカルロス剛が学んだ技術が、のちにメキシコで一家の事業拡大に役立つことになる。

春日光子の生涯　THE LIFE OF MITSUKO KASUGA　195

Inao and Carlos Tsuyoshi went to Japan by sea
伊那雄とカルロス剛が日本へ渡った船

Carlos Tsuyoshi as a foreign student in Japan (Third lef)
日本留学中の長男・カルロス剛（左から三人目）

Carlos Tsuyoshi learned vinyl manufacturing in a Japanese factory.
カルロス剛がアルバイトとしてビニール加工を学んだ日本の会社

12. FULL-SCALE BUSINESS EXPANSION

Tanka 031

事業の拡大

In 1956, Tsutomu, together with friends, built a factory to make celluloid toys and fountain pens. Believing that this kind of product had a promising future, he modeled the factory facilities on Japanese technology. Carlos Tsuyoshi's return from Japan after learning about plastic processing proved timely and led to a collaboration between father and son in the plastic toy manufacturing business.

Tsutomu was extremely busy as he worked to expand his business ventures. He was managing two confectionery stores, making and selling dried apricots, and producing and selling plastic toys.

Tsutomu was particularly busy during the last two weeks of spring every year, when apricots were delivered to his factory. During those times he would wake up at 6 a.m., and open the factory by 7 a.m. to receive raw material shipments. After measuring the apricots, he'd transfer them to barrels and rush off to the confectionary. Going between two stores to

The vinyl toys made big seccesses
ビニール製おもちゃは次々とヒットした

1956年、勉はメキシコシティで、セルロイドのおもちゃや万年筆を作る工場を建てる。将来性があると見込んで仲間と一緒に始めた事業だった。工場の設備は日本の技術を土台にしていた。そこに、日本に留学させていた長男・カルロス剛が、ビニール加工の仕事を覚えて戻ってきた。勉とカルロス剛は親子で協力して、この工場でビニール玩具の製造も始めることにした。

こうして仕事をどんどん広げる勉の毎日は、多忙を極めていた。二軒の菓子屋の経営。干しアンズの製造・販売。そこにセルロイドやビニールの玩具の生産・販売が加わったのである。

アンズの仕入れは毎年、晩春の二週間くらいが勝負だったので、その時期はとりわけ忙しかった。朝6時に起き、7時には干しアンズ工場を開けて、材料となるアンズを生産者から受け取る。アンズの計量を終えて樽につけ込んだら、今度は菓子屋に駆けつける。二軒の店

manage product orders and payments, he would eat the lunch Mitsuko prepared for him before heading off to deliver plastic toys. He would then go to the toy factory to provide instructions to the production line workers. As the sun was setting, he would return to the confectionary to confirm sales for the day. After closing the store's doors around 10 p.m., he would see the female workers to their homes before finally returning home himself. Such was the lifestyle of Tsutomu Kasuga. Even after returning home, he would keep working, often immersing himself in studying new machinery arrivals from Japan. He never made it to bed before 1 a.m.

Mitsuko also worked constantly to support such the hardworking Tsutomu. However, despite her tireless efforts to share the workload, Tsutomu was afflicted with chronic fatigue.

舗をまわって商品の注文や支払いを済ませ、光子が持たせてくれた弁当を口の中にかき込んだら、次はビニール玩具の商品の配達だ。その後おもちゃ工場に移動し、生産ラインに立つ従業員たちに指示。日が沈む頃、再び菓子屋に戻って一日の売れ行きを確認。10時に店のシャッターを閉めた後、女性店員たちをそれぞれの家に送り届けながら、やっと帰宅するという生活である。さらに家に戻ってからも、日本から届いた新しい機械の研究に没頭。いつもベッドに入るときには深夜の1時を過ぎていた。

このような多忙な日々が何年も続く勉を、光子は必死で支えた。しかし、寝る間も惜しんで働き続ける勉の体は、知らぬ間にすり減っていったのである。

Looking after the store
菓子屋で店番をする娘

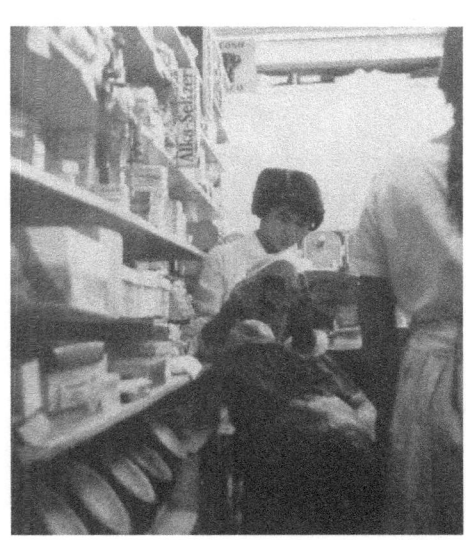

Tsutomu with *chamoys*
天日干しされるチャモイと勉

13. AN EXTENDED FAMILY

Tanka 008, 010, 011, 020, 050

大所帯

Tsutomu never forgot the times he received help from fellow Japanese immigrants when he was younger, and he made a point of paying it forward to young people trying to make their way. Tsutomu let young workers stay at his home and taught them skills that would help them succeed. It was not uncommon for there to be several additions to the family at dinner or bedtime.

Mitsuko always ensured that there was enough food to feed at least ten people every day. Mitsuko's daily routine consisted of leaving for the market early in the morning, where she filled two large baskets with vegetables and meat and returning home to start cooking for the day's meals. The dishes she prepared were so large they overflowed from pots and skillets, but were nonetheless devoured by the end of the day.

Mitsuko's natural curiosity was an advantage in the kitchen. In the same way that she had committed to learning about and understanding Mexican culture, she devoted that same attention and care to the country's cuisine.

Mitsuko and Tsutomu
welcomed everyone into their home
誰でも家族同様に
迎え入れた勉と光子

　勉は、自分が若い頃に日本人移民の先輩たちに世話になった恩を忘れず、頼って来る若者がいればいつでも喜んで受け入れた。その若者の経歴などには頓着せず、自分の家に住まわせては仕事を教え、その成長を後押しした。そんなわけで勉と光子の家には、何人もの住み込みの従業員や書生がいた。

　昼食のときには、家族に加えて従業員や書生も一緒に食卓を囲むのが常で、光子はおよそ10人分の食事を日々用意しなければならなかった。朝になるとすぐ市場に出かけ、特大のかご二つを野菜や肉でいっぱいにして戻るのが光子の日課だった。大きな鍋やフライパンにあふれるほど作った料理は、その日のうちにきれいに空っぽになった。

　光子は料理上手だった。メキシコの文化を積極的に吸収しようとする光子の好奇心は、メキシコ料理の習得にも役立ったようだ。市場に行くたび、野菜や調味料を売るメキシコ人たちに調理法を尋ね、そこに独自の工夫を加えてレシピを改良していく。こんなふうに研究を

At the market, Mitsuko would ask produce and spice vendors how to use different ingredients and then she would add her unique perspective to make the recipes her own. Mitsuko's take on *mole poblano* (a famous Mexican stew dish) had a reputation for tasting more authentic than the version made by Mexico City locals.

familiar faces grow,
as do the words
we exchange.
the morning market
is my delight.
—Akane

Mitsuko
光子

重ねて作られた光子のモレ（メキシコを代表する煮込み料理）は、メキシコ人が作るよりもメキシコらしい味わいだと評判になるほどだった。

　　　　　顔見知りふえて物云い交し合う朝の市場に行くが楽しく
　　　　　　　　　　　　　　　　　　　　　　　　　—あかね

　大所帯の春日家には、さらに小動物もたくさんいた。家で飼っていたのは、コンゴウインコ1羽、オオハシ1羽、タヌキ1匹、オウム2羽、犬2匹、七面鳥3羽、ウサギ4匹、カメ5匹、猫11匹、アヒル12羽。さらに鳩や魚なども数多くいて、庭はさながら春日動物園といった様相を呈していた。光子が料理するときにできる野菜くずなどは、残らずこの小さな同居人たちの餌となった。

　勉はこの時期に、日本からブレスレットや髪飾りを輸入する仕事も始めている。商品の売れ行きは上々だった。勉は、すでに軌道に乗った菓子屋の経営は人に任せて、おもちゃ工場

The Kasuga household also had a lot of pets. At one point, they had a parrot, a toucan, a raccoon, two owls, two dogs, three turkeys, four rabbits, five turtles, eleven cats, twelve ducks, several doves, and many fish. The garden was dubbed the Kasuga zoo. Mitsuko used vegetable scraps from cooking as feed for these animals.

Around this time, Tsutomu began importing bracelets and hair accessories from Japan. These products quickly grew in popularity. With business at the confectionaries stable, Tsutomu delegated its daily operations and focused on managing the toy factory and expanding their other businesses.

The family assorting bracelets
家族みんなで
ブレスレットの仕分け

など、他の事業に集中してビジネスを拡大していった。

204   PART II   第二部

14. PAST AND FUTURE MEET IN JAPAN

Tanka 017–019, 022, 023, 055–058

日本とのつながり

春日光子の生涯　THE LIFE OF MITSUKO KASUGA　205

By 1960, the family's economic situation was finally stable, so Tsutomu felt comfortable planning a visit to Japan. It was the first time he'd see his home country in 30 years. Tsutomu's parents had already passed away, but his many siblings were looking forward to the reunion.

While visiting his siblings and relatives, Tsutomu realized that things were not going well for his younger brother Toru. Like Tsutomu, Toru had suspended his education when their father passed away leaving the family in financial distress.

As was typical of Tsutomu, he immediately started pondering how he could help his brother. It occurred to him that there could be a market for imported Mexican opals in Japan. At the time, rainbow-colored opals were growing in popularity in Japan, so as soon as Tsutomu returned to Mexico, he found an opal producer with whom to make a deal.

This opal business quickly took off. In fact, the opals

Tooru, younger brother of Tsutomu
勉の弟・亨

一家の収入が安定してきた 1960 年、勉は初めて祖国日本に一時帰国した。メキシコに移住してから実に 30 年の月日が流れていた。勉の両親は既に亡くなっていたが、大勢のきょうだいが勉に会うのを楽しみに待っていた。

日本できょうだいや親類を訪ねてまわるうち、勉は、弟・亨の暮らし向きがよくないことを知った。昔、父が若くして他界し家に借金ができたときに、勉と同じように進学をあきらめなければならなかった弟であった。

何とか弟を助けてやれないかと考えて思いついたのが、メキシコで産出するオパールの宝石を日本に輸出し販売するというビジネスだった。当時日本では、虹色に輝くオパールの人気が高まっていた。勉はメキシコに戻るとすぐに、オパールの生産者を探して契約をした。

このオパール貿易は、間を置かずして軌道に乗った。やがて供給が追いつかないほどの大ヒットとなり、目利き・仕入れ担当の勉にも、予想以上の大きな収入をもたらすこととなった。

勉の一時帰国に続いて、1962 年には光子も里帰りの機会を得た。ほぼ 27 年ぶりに踏みしめるふるさとの土だった。7 年ぶりに再会した父は、思っていた以上に老いていた。光子

were so popular that they had a supply problem, resulting in great profit for Tsutomu, who was in charge of selection and inventory.

After Tsutomu's trip to Japan, Mitsuko had the opportunity to return home in 1962. It had been nearly 27 years since she'd last seen her hometown. Her father, whom she had not seen in seven years, had aged much more than expected. And in reuniting with her siblings, Mitsuko rejoiced with those doing well and empathized with those who were having difficulties.

As the country prepared to host the Tokyo Olympics in two years, Japan was in the midst of a period of rapid economic development. Mitsuko was surprised by speed at which the country was changing. While the quality of life had increased significantly for most people, she feared that Japan was on the verge of losing many of its traditional values. Overwhelmed by complex emotions, Mitsuko returned to Mexico where

Luis Takeshi
東京水産大学で学んだ次男・ルイス毅

の姉妹は、幸せそうな者もいれば戦後苦しい生活をしている者もいて、それぞれの運命をたどっていた。

2年後に東京オリンピックをひかえた日本は、高度経済成長の真っただ中にあって、急激なスピードで変貌をとげていた。光子はそんな祖国の姿に驚きながらも、「生活が豊かになる一方で、失われつつある大切なものがたくさんある」と感じた。複雑な思いを胸に、光子は夫と子どもたちの待つメキシコへと戻った。

この時期に春日夫妻は、子どもたちを次々とメキシコから送り出し、急成長する日本で学ばせている。次男のルイス毅（たけし）と三女のエスペランサ真佐子は東京水産大学（現・東京海洋大学）で学び、卒業後はメキシコに戻って水産加工などの仕事を始めた。他の子どもたちも全員が日本へと送られ、それぞれに日本の文化や日本語を学ぶ機会を得た。勉がいくつもの事業を手がけて稼いだお金の多くは、子ども六人の学費と旅費にあてられたのだった。

her husband and children awaited.

Tsutomu and Mitsuko gradually sent all of their children to study Japanese language and culture in a rapidly growing Japan. Their second son, Luis Takeshi, and third daughter, Esperanza Masako, studied at the Tokyo University of Fisheries (currently, the Tokyo University of Marine Science and Technology). After graduating, they returned to Mexico to work in fish processing and related businesses. Most of the money Tsutomu made from all his business ventures went towards the educational expenses of his children.

my son
devotes his life to
the Mexican sea.
may his sincerity be delivered
to the sea gods.
—Akane

メキシコの海一筋に生きる子の真心とゞけ海神の許
—あかね

Hiking with 8-mm VCR in Mitsuko's hand
8ミリカメラを手に持ち娘四人とハイキングへ

春日光子の生涯　THE LIFE OF MITSUKO KASUGA　209

15. GRANDCHILDREN ARRIVE

Tanka 021, 051, 052, 066–074

孫の誕生

Mitsuko was 47 years old when her oldest daughter, Ermelinda Michiko, married. A mere year later, Ermelinda's daughter was born, filling Mitsuko with great joy.

Soon after that, Carlos Tsuyoshi married Masako, a woman from Mitsuko's hometown of Ina. Mitsuko was very proud that the family was welcoming a bride from Japan. Mitsuko often enjoyed making Nagano *miso* paste and pickled vegetables in the traditional way of their hometown with her daughter-in-law. She even mentioned this on multiple occasions in her tanka.

From Masako's perspective, as a new bride in a foreign land, Mitsuko was probably a very strict mother-in-law. Mitsuko required that she be a traditional wife and strong mother who could support the Kasuga family through good times and

With their first grandchild
初孫を抱く

光子が47歳になった年、長女のエルメリンダ美智子が結婚。翌年には女の子が生まれた。初孫を抱く光子の喜びは大変なものであった。

続いて、長男のカルロス剛が、光子と同じ信州・伊那出身の女性正子（まさこ）と結婚した。日本からメキシコにお嫁さんを迎えられたことを、光子は誇りに思った。同郷の正子とともに信州味噌を仕込んだり、ぬか漬けを作ったりするひと時のことは、たびたび短歌にも詠まれている。

メキシコに嫁いできた正子にとって、光子は強く厳格な姑であっただろう。「あなたが春日の家を支えていくのだからしっかりしなさい」と、光子は正子に昔ながらの「よい妻」「よい母」であることを求めた。かつてふるさとで、祖母が嫁である母・ゆきえに対して厳しく接する様子を見て育った光子は、他のやり方を知らなかったともいえる。

長男の結婚を機に、光子たち夫婦は長男夫婦といっしょに大きな屋敷に引っ越した。新しい住まいは広々としていて、寝室だけでも五部屋を数えた。家の裏手には将来、工場を建て

bad. Of course, Mitsuko's only role model for a mother-in-law was her own grandmother, who had always been very strict towards her mother, so she likely behaved accordingly.

Their eldest son's wedding gave Mitsuko and Tsutomu the opportunity to move into a larger house with their son and his new wife. The new home was a spacious five bedroom structure located on a plot of land large enough to build a factory in the future. The success of the opal trade had finally provided the Kasuga family with a financially secure, comfortable way of life.

The new house had a Buddhist altar next to a portrait of Our Lady of Guadalupe (Mexico's patron Virgin Mary). These representations were Mitsuko's way of honoring both Japan and Mexico for the blessings they had provided her family. She believed that the

Carlos Tsuyoshi with his fiancee Masako
長男・カルロス剛と結婚相手の正子

ることができる大きな空き地もあった。オパールの貿易事業が大成功をおさめたおかげで、一家の暮らしはぐっと豊かになっていた。

屋敷の一室には、仏壇とグアダルーペ（メキシコの聖母）の肖像画が飾られた。今日の一家があるのは日本のおかげであり、またメキシコのおかげでもあるのだという、光子の感謝の念の表れである。光子は、日本の伝統もメキシコの伝統もどちらもなくてはならない自分の一部なのだと思い、大切にしていた。そんな母の姿を見て育った六人の子どもたちは、自分が日系メキシコ人として多様な文化の中に暮らしていることに自然と誇りを感じるようになった。豊かな文化を育みながら、一家は年輪を重ねていった。

　　　　　裸木の隣りに芽吹く樹黄ばむ木もありてメヒコの年暮れむとす
　　　　　　　　　　　　　　　　　　　　　　　　　　　　　　　—あかね

引っ越しの後、長男夫婦に男の子が生まれた。「Kasuga」の姓をメキシコの地に受け継い

traditions of both Japan and Mexico were a vital part of who she was. Her six children had grown up proud of being Japanese Mexicans and part of a diverse culture. As time went by, the Kasuga family had developed their own unique traditions, which drew from both cultures.

a naked tree,
alongside one with blossoms,
and another tinged in yellow.
such is Mexico
nearing year's end.

—Akane

With six grown-up children
成人した六人の子と

でくれるであろう初めての男孫の誕生に、光子は満足していた。春日家では、その後も次々と孫にめぐまれた。22歳の若さで親きょうだいから離れてメキシコにやって来た光子にとって、自分の血を分けた人間が増えていくことは、価値観を共有する仲間が増えていくことのようで頼もしく思えた。

　日系三世メキシコ人として生きてゆく孫の世代に、光子は大きな期待をかけていた。その気持ちは幼い子どもたちにとっては、時に重すぎるプレッシャーとなった。孫たちに、日本人としてもメキシコ人としても完璧な人間になることを期待した光子。特に言葉遣いや態度にはうるさく、「おばあちゃん」の前ではできるだけ日本語を話すように求めたという。生まれたときからスペイン語の環境の中で育っている孫たちにとって、それは決して簡単なことではない。中には、「おばあちゃん」から小言を言われるのが嫌で、光子を避ける孫もいた。孫たちにとって光子は、怖くて近寄りがたい存在であったと言える。光子は、孫への愛情が深ければ深いほど、かえって厳しく接した。「おじいちゃん」の勉が孫を抱いたりなでたりして可愛がったのとは、対照的な姿であった。

Carlos Tsuyoshi's wife gave birth to a baby boy soon after the family moved to the larger house. Mitsuko was ecstatic at the birth of a grandson, the first boy who would carry the Kasuga family name in Mexico into the next generation. In short order, the Kasuga family was blessed with many more grandchildren.

Since Mitsuko had left her family at a young age, welcoming children of her bloodline into the world also meant welcoming people who would share her values. Mitsuko had high expectations of her grandchildren, who were third-generation Japanese-Mexicans. Mitsuko expected them to be

Mitsuko and Tsutomu
surrounded by their grandchildren
孫たちに囲まれる光子と勉

　　人類が月に足跡遺す時七人目の孫我家に生る

　　　　　　　　　　　　　　　　　　　　―あかね

perfectly Japanese and perfectly Mexican, which could sometimes be a heavy burden for such small shoulders. Mitsuko was particularly strict regarding speech and behavior, and she expected the children to speak Japanese in her presence, which was challenging for children who were born and raised in a Spanish-language environment. Some of the grandchildren even avoided Mitsuko because they were scared of her and didn't want to be the recipients of her demands. For Mitsuko, however, such strictness was the manifestation of her devotion to her grandchildren. The more she loved them, the stricter she became. This was a marked contrast from grandpa Tsutomu, who doted on his grandchildren.

> *as human footprints*
> *are impressed*
> *on the moon*
> *the seventh grandchild*
> *joins our family.*
>
> —Akane

春日光子の生涯　THE LIFE OF MITSUKO KASUGA　215

At the wedding of Carlos Tsuyoshi, the special guest was Toshiro Mifune, a famous actor of Japan (second left in the fromt row)
長男の結婚式には、俳優の三船敏郎夫妻（前列左端）も出席。メキシコで映画の撮影が行われた時に春日家が三船敏郎の世話をしたのがきっかけで、親交が深まった。

Tsutomu at the construction site of his factory
工場建設の現場に立つ勉（右）

16. MEXICAN PRIDE

Tanka 041–043, 059, 060

メキシコの誇り

In the summer of 1968, Mexico was bustling with the excitement of hosting the Summer Olympics.

Balloons and banners produced at Tsutomu's plastic plant lined the streets leading up to the Olympic stadium with brilliant flashes of color. Mitsuko glanced proudly at their products, which bore the official logo of the Mexico Olympics. They seemed to her a metaphor for the family's own prosperity at the time.

Further establishing the Kasuga family as an important name in Mexico, their children Luis Takeshi and María Teresa Miwako accompanied Mexican

The giantic Olympic rings for the opening ceremony were made at Tsutomu's factory.
メキシコオリンピックの開会式で空に放たれた五輪の形の巨大バルーンは勉の会社で作ったものだった

1968年夏、メキシコはオリンピックに沸いていた。

勉の工場で作られたビニール製のバルーンやバナーが、スタジアムに続く大通りとオリンピック会場を華やかに彩った。メキシコオリンピックの公式ロゴが入った自分たちの製品を、光子は誇らしい気持ちで見つめた。ビジネスは好調だった。

1970年には次男のルイス毅と末娘のマリアテレサ美和子が、メキシコのエチェベリア大統領夫妻に付き添い、秘書兼日本語通訳として訪日した。それをきっかけに、光子たち春日ファミリーとエチェベリア大統領夫妻との親交が深まった。メキシコ国立宮殿で開かれる国家のセレモニーに出席するよう家族みんなで招待されたことは、光子にとって大きな栄誉を感じる出来事だった。

「移民として極貧からスタートした自分たちが、ついにメキシコという国に認められたのだ」

感慨にふける光子の胸に、様々な思い出が去来した。

President Luis Echeverría and the first lady as secretaries and interpreters on a visit to Japan in 1970. This trip built a close bond between the Kasugas and the first family. Mitsuko was very proud when the entire family was invited to a national ceremony held at Mexico's national palace.

"We came here as poor immigrants, and we are now being recognized by Mexico." Such an honor made Mitsuko feel simultaneously grateful and proud.

"viva México!"
our President
and the crowd

The president Echeverría (on the right) in Tsutomu's factory
エチェベリア大統領（右）を
工場に案内する勉

ビバメヒコ大統領と群衆の声の和す時 涙 湧き出ず

——あかね

光子の六人の子どもはそれぞれ立派に成長し、一人また一人と結婚・独立していった。1972年には、一番末の娘が結婚。子どもたち全員が巣立ったその年、光子の父・伊那雄が90歳で他界したという知らせが届いた。光子は57歳になっていた。

ある日、勉は子どもたちを集めた。
真剣な面持ちで勉が話したのは、オパールの貿易事業から手を引くという計画だった。家族はみんな不思議がった。事業は絶好調だったからだ。
勉の考えはこうだった。「若いうちは皆、額に汗して働いたほうがいい。オパールの事業によって簡単に経済的な成功が手に入ってしまうと、まだ若いおまえたちは人生の目的を見失うかもしれない。」

shouted in unison.
my tears welled up.
—Akane

The year 1972 was a bittersweet year for Mitsuko. Her last daughter married that year, meaning that all six of her children were now settled. She took great pride in their independence and strength. It was this same year, however, that Mitsuko's father passed away, at the age of 90. Mitsuko was 57 years old.

One day, Tsutomu gathered his adult children and explained that he planned to pull out of the opal trade. This came as a surprise to his family,

Mitsuko and the family of María Teresa with the president Echeverría (center)
エチェベリア大統領夫妻（中央）、末娘・マリアテレサ美和子の家族と光子

　勉はその言葉の通り、オパール貿易仲介の仕事をきっぱりとやめた。日本でオパールの販売を担当していた弟の亨(とおる)には、今後は直接メキシコの業者のところに買い付けに行くようにと頼んだ。
　六人の子どもたちが既に独立した今、勉の関心は経済的な成功よりも、社会貢献に移っていた。勉には夢があったのだ。日系人とメキシコ人がともに学べる、小中高一貫の学校をメキシコに作ることである。学校建設の実現のために、勉はパンフレットを作ったり、日本の大臣に会って援助要請をしたりして、全力で取り組んでいた。光子は、理想に燃えて突き進む勉を心から尊敬し、誰よりも応援していた。

since the business was doing extremely well. But Tsutomu explained his reasoning, "All of you should learn the importance of hard work while you are young. If we stay in the opal business, you would attain economic success too easily and may lose sight of how to lead a purposeful life."

Tsutomu asked his younger brother Toru, who was handling the Japan side of the business, to work directly with the Mexican producers. Then, as promised, he severed ties to the opal business.

As his six children had all become independent, Tsutomu's thoughts turned from economic success to social contribution. Tsutomu dreamed of building a Japanese school where Japanese descendants and Mexican children could learn together at the elementary, junior, and high school levels. Tsutomu worked hard to achieve this dream, including preparing pamphlets to request support from Japanese ministers. Even though Mitsuko was more of a pragmatist than Tsutomu, she greatly respected his idealism and passion and was his greatest supporter in this dream.

Tsutomu's company produced various baloons with the logo of Mexico City Olympics
さまざまな色、形のオリンピックロゴ入りバルーンを多数製造

The main street to the Olympic stadium was decorated with banners made at Tsutomu's factory
オリンピック会場へ続く通りに勉の会社で作ったバナーがたなびいた

17. DEATH COMES SUDDENLY

Tanka 078–096

夫の急逝

During one of the most fulfilling periods of her life, Mitsuko was suddenly dealt life's greatest blow. In March 1973, Tsutomu was taken to the hospital after the sudden onset of severe stomach pain. He passed away two days later, at the age of 62, from acute pancreatitis.

Tsutomu's hospital room echoed with his daughters' unconsolable cries. To everyone's surprise, Mitsuko did not cry. She politely thanked doctors and nurses, and calmly went about gathering their belongings in the hospital room. This image of the unbreakable, dry-eyed mother was branded in Ermelinda Michiko's memory. "She was like a female *samurai*," Mitsuko's oldest daughter would recall.

After Tsutomu's funeral, Mitsuko spread half of his ashes on Mount Popocatépetl as specified in his will. This famous volcano can be seen from anywhere in Mexico City and

Tsutomu and Mitsuko
勉と光子

1973年3月、充実した日々を過ごしていた光子に、人生最大の悲劇が起こる。

それはあまりに突然のことだった。おなかがひどく痛むと言って病院に運ばれた夫の勉が、そのたった二日後にこの世を去ってしまったのだ。急性すい炎だった。勉62歳の、あまりに若すぎる逝去である。

病室は、嘆き悲しむ娘たちの泣き声に包まれた。しかし、なぜか光子の目に涙はなかった。医師や看護師に丁寧に礼を述べ、落ち着き払った様子で病室の物を片付けていた母の姿を、長女のエルメリンダ美智子が覚えている。涙をまったく見せない気丈な姿は、まるで女サムライのようだったという。

葬儀を済ませた光子は、勉の生前の希望にしたがって、遺灰の半分をポポカテペトル山にまいた。ポポカテペトル山（通称・ポポ）はメキシコシティのどこからでも見える大きな火山で、日系移民の間では「メキシコ富士」と呼ばれ親しまれている。勉の遺灰は、山小屋から見上げたところにある岩場の一本松を中心にまかれた。この散骨のセレモニーには、勉の早すぎる死を惜しむ数多くの親類や友人たちが集まった。

is known among Japanese immigrants as Mexico's Mount Fuji. Tsutomu's ashes were spread around a lone pine tree that grew among rocks near the mountain lodge. The ceremony to spread his ashes was attended by many relatives and close friends who mourned his sudden departure.

In May, two months after her husband's sudden death, Mitsuko took his remaining ashes and visited Ina to place his ashes in Tsutomu's family grave. While there, Mitsuko made the rounds with family members, still not fully absorbing her husband's death.

> *turned to bones,*
> *my husband*
> *returns home.*
> *sing tenderly,*
> *uguisu.*
> —Akane

　夫が急逝してから二か月後、光子は残りの遺灰を抱えて伊那を訪れた。勉の故郷のお墓に分骨するためだった。夫の死にまだ現実味を感じられないまま、光子は日本の親類へのあいさつまわりをした。

　　骨となり故郷へ帰る我が夫(つま)にやさしく鳴けよ藪(やぶ)のうぐいす
　　　　　　　　　　　　　　　　　　　　　　　　　　　　　—あかね

　光子の様子が変わったのは、この伊那での弔いが終わり、メキシコでの日常が再び始まった頃だった。娘たちはこの時期、光子が泣き崩れる姿をたびたび目にしている。一連の法要が終わって、張りつめていた気持ちを支えるものがなくなったのであろう。やっと涙を流せるようになった光子は、夫の死という受け入れがたい現実の中で一人もがいていた。36年余りにわたってともに人生を切り開いてきたパートナーを、突然失った光子。その悲しみ、嘆きは想像に尽くせない。

(*Uguisu* is a bird loved by Japansese. Its distinctive breeding call can be heard in spring in Japan.)

It wasn't until Mitsuko returned to Mexico from funerary events in Japan that the emotional dam broke. Dealing with the details of death had, in some ways, kept its harsh reality contained. Once all relevant matters were settled, Mitsuko was left with the hardest task of all: returning to the routine of daily life. It was surreal to her that the partner with whom she built a life for 36 years had suddenly vanished. She was so overcome with grief and despair that her daughters often witnessed their stoic mother break down into tears.

Mt. Popocatépetl
ポポカテペトル山

　夫に先立たれ、心に大きな穴があいたように感じていた頃だった。光子はふと思い立って、自分の短歌一首を朝日新聞の短歌投稿欄「朝日歌壇」に送ってみた。自信がないまま投稿した歌であったが、それが思いがけず優秀作の一つとして選ばれて紙上に掲載される。60歳のときのことである。

　以来、光子は生涯にわたって投稿を続け、合わせて五十首の短歌と五句の俳句が朝日新聞で発表された。自分の歌が選ばれたのを知るたび、生きてゆく力が沸いてくるのを感じる光子であった。

　夫・勉の死から4年後の1977年。光子は、日本メキシコ学院（通称：リセオ）の開校セレモニーに出席していた。勉が夢見ていた、メキシコ人と日系人がともに学べる小中高一貫の学校設立が、ついに実現したのである。

　この日本メキシコ学院は、多くの日系人の願いと努力の結晶であった。メキシコシティには、かつて光子が自宅で開いていたような私設の日本語塾がいくつかあったが、それらが統合されて日本メキシコ学院の土台となったのである。開校にあたっては、日本政府、日本の

Her husband's death left a permanent wound in Mitsuko's heart. But life did not stop for her and she needed to find strength where she could. Giving herself over to writing was one way for her to find a small measure of joy. On an occasion when she felt particularly bold and inspired, Mitsuko submitted a tanka to the *"Asahi Kadan* (tanka section)" of the *Asahi Shimbun* newspaper. Mitsuko wasn't very optimistic about her chances, but, to her surprise, her poem was selected for publication. Mitsuko was 60 years old at the time.

Mitsuko would go on to submit dozens of poems and, over time, 50 of her tanka and haiku were published in the *Asahi Shimbun*. Mitsuko found the strength to keep going every time a poem of hers was chosen for publication.

Carlos Tsuyoshi looking at the construction site of the *Liceo Mexicano Japonés*
建設中の日本メキシコ学院を見守る長男・カルロス剛

商社、在留日系人の寄付が大きな力となった。また、この学校設立は、父・勉の遺志を継ごうと誓った六人の子らが奔走し、二世を中心として日系人コミュニティーをたばねた成果でもあった。光子は日本メキシコ学院の誕生を、人一倍喜んだ。

　　　ポポの嶺ゆ亡夫視てあらん今日の日に大統領は基石置き給う
　　　　　　　　　　　　　　　　　　　　　　　　　　　　　—あかね

「日本とメキシコの文化交流」を教育理念に掲げ、日本語を必修科目とするユニークなこの学校は、その後大統領の子息も通うほどの名門校となった。現在も、メキシコシティ内の高校総合評価で上位にランクインし続けており、日系人の教育という勉の夢を越えて、広くメキシコ社会全体に貢献している。光子の孫やひ孫の多くも、この学校の卒業生となった。

In 1977, four years after the death of her husband, Mitsuko attended the opening ceremony of a Japanese-Mexican School (commonly referred to as a *liceo*). Tsutomu's dream of an elementary, middle, and high school for both Mexicans and Japanese descendants had finally become a reality. Until then, Mexico City had several home-based Japanese schools like the one Mitsuko once ran. The new school had brought many of these small schools together into a formal program.

The Japanese government, several Japanese trading companies and the Japanese immigrant community were all involved in building the school. Also, driven by the promise to fulfill their father's dying wish, Tsutomu's six children worked tirelessly to make the school a reality. And yet, among all the people rejoicing at the school's opening ceremony, you'd be hard-pressed to find someone happier than Mitsuko.

春日光子の生涯   THE LIFE OF MITSUKO KASUGA   227

> *my late husband*
> *must be watching from the peak of Popo*
> *as today is the day*
> *our President*
> *laid the foundation stone.*
> —Akane

Based on the educational principle of cultural exchange between Japan and Mexico, the school was unique in that it made Japanese language a requirement. The school would grow so prestigious that the Mexican president's son was once a student and, to this day, it ranks among the top high schools in Mexico City. Tsutomu's dream of joining Japanese immigrants with Mexican students was surpassed as the school grew to contribute more broadly to Mexican society. It would have pleased Tsutomu greatly to know that his and Mitsuko's grandchildren and great-grandchildren would be alumni of this school.

Liceo Mexicano Japonés
— Opening ceremony
日本メキシコ学院開校記念式典

A shool that fosters both
Japanese and Mexican cultures
メキシコと日本の文化を
融合させた教育を目指す

18. CREATIVE MATURITY

Tanka 024–028, 044, 053, 063, 064, 075–077, 097, 098

歌人としての成熟

春日光子の生涯　THE LIFE OF MITSUKO KASUGA

In 1985, a tanka submitted from Mexico was selected for excellence at a poetry event in Japan's Imperial Palace. After receiving notification from the Imperial Household Agency, Mitsuko immediately went to her husband's portrait to share the good news.

> *spent one day*
> *of my trip to Bali*
> *in the furrows of a field*
> *catching river snails*
> *with children from the village.*
> —Akane

The Imperial Palace poetry events are based on themes that change every year. That year's theme was "journey." Mitsuko's poem was written about a vacation trip to Bali she and Tsutomu took with their daughters, who were studying in Japan at the time.

　1985年。宮中歌会始の詠進歌としてメキシコから投稿した光子の短歌が、見事佳作として選ばれた。宮内庁から入選を知らせる手紙を受けとった光子は、真っ先に勉の遺影のところに持っていって喜びを報告したという。

　これが歌会始で佳作に選ばれた短歌である。

　　　バリ島の旅の一日を田の畦に村の童とたにし拾ひぬ
　　　　　　　　　　　　　　　　　　　　　　　　—あかね

　宮中歌会始では毎年異なるお題が出されるが、この年のテーマは、「旅」であった。この光子の短歌は、時間と空間を越えた心の旅が詠まれた一首である。
　歌の題材となっているのは、日本に留学中だった二人の娘を連れて、光子と勉が東南アジアのバリへ旅行に行ったときの体験である。タニシとは田んぼによく住む巻貝の一種で、光子のふるさと信州では、味噌汁に入れて食べることもあるなじみ深いものだった。バリの田

As a child, Mitsuko often ate *miso* soup made with river snails found in rice fields. Walking through Bali's rice fields, Mitsuko remembered the fun times she had gathering these snails as a child. There had likely been friendly competitions between Mitsuko and her sisters and friends to collect the most snails.

"I've already found twenty."

"Ha! I have thirty. I win!"

Mitsuko's tanka captured the spiritual journey that transcended space and time as memories of her own childhood overlay her adult experience of Bali's rice fields.

The Japan of Mitsuko's childhood was never far from her mind, whether she was on vacation in Southeast Asia or in Mexico surrounded by her children and grandchildren. Even a half-century after leaving her hometown, her love for Ina never dissipated and fond memories popped into her mind, and writing, frequently.

園を歩く光子の胸に、自分が子どもの頃にタニシ拾いをした楽しい思い出が鮮やかによみがえってきたのであろう。光子もかつて、姉妹や友だちと競うようにして「もう二十個集めたよ」「私は三十個。勝った！」などとやっていたのかもしれない。

東南アジアを旅するときも、メキシコの家で子どもたちに囲まれているときも、光子の胸にはいつも懐かしいふるさとがあった。日本を離れて半世紀がたっても、郷愁が消えることはなかったのである。

百合の根に似たる味するユカの花 鉄鍋に煮る雨の一日を

—あかね

長年にわたって日系コミュニティーに貢献してきた功績により光子が勲六等瑞宝章を授与されたのは、詠進歌の入選から２年後のことであった。光子は72歳になっていた。

当時、光子の六人の子どもたちは働き盛り。それぞれに水産加工業、おもちゃや食品の製

> *yucca flower,*
> *similar in taste to*
> *lily root,*
> *simmering in an iron pot*
> *on this rainy day.*
> —Akane

Two years after her poem's selection by the Imperial Palace, Mitsuko was awarded the Order of the Sacred Treasure, Sixth Class, for her many contributions to the Japanese community. Mitsuko was 72 years old.

By then, her six children were all hard-working adults involved in various industries, including fisheries, toy and food manufacturing and sales.

Mitsuko was living in Mexico City with her eldest son's family, but she greatly enjoyed visiting her children and grandchildren, who had spread out

---

造・販売などを手がけ、奮闘していた。各地で頑張っている子どもたちと、かわいい孫たちを訪ねていくのは光子の大きな楽しみだった。

光子は普段メキシコシティで長男一家と一緒に暮らしていたが、機会があれば、市内に住む次女のマルタ悠紀子と時間を過ごした。また、まとまった時間があると、他の子どもたちが住むマサトラン、レオン、ラパスの町や、アメリカのワシントンＤＣなどに飛んで行った。

こうした小旅行の中でも、三女のエスペランサ真佐子を訪ねるときには特別の楽しみがあった。真佐子は、太平洋岸にあるマサトランの町で夫とともに水産加工の工場を営んでいたが、そこで一緒に働くのが光子にとって幸せなひと時だったのである。体を動かして仕事をすると、気持ちに張りが出た。海のない信州に生まれ育った自分が、太平洋に面したマサトランの町で、エビや魚に囲まれて働いているという運命のめぐりあわせが、光子には愉快に感じられた。

子どもたちを訪ねて回る小旅行は、光子に格好の詩作のチャンスを与えた。なかでもマサトランで詠まれた短歌が数多く残されている。

to live in various places. Whenever possible, she spent time with her daughter Marta Yukiko, who also lived in the city. And she would take longer vacations to see her children living in Mazatlán, León, La Paz, and Washington D.C. in the U.S.

Among these vacations, she was particularly fond of trips to visit Esperanza Masako. Esperanza Masako lived with her husband in the Pacific Coast town of Mazatlán, where they owned a fish-processing business. Staying active fitted Mitsuko's personality, so she loved working with them when she visited. For the young girl from landlocked Nagano, working in this Mexican port town surrounded by shrimp and fish was a pleasant twist

Mitsuko happily working
in the fish processing factory
水産加工の工場でいきいきと働く光子

漁師等の喜怒哀楽は陸におき海は太古のまゝの音する

—あかね

湖に群れ飛ぶかもめの中をとぶ白蝶一羽どこ迄もとぶ

—あかね

好奇心旺盛だった光子は、積極的に海外旅行も楽しんだ。自分がかつてメキシコに移住したとき、30日もの間船に揺られてやっと太平洋を横断したことを思えば、飛行機に乗ってたったの一日で世界のあちこちに行けるというのは、ありがたいことであった。

光子は自分の子どもや友人とともに、スペイン、イギリス、フランス、ドイツ、スイス、ベトナム、ホンジュラスなどを訪ねている。旅先の土地で光子が必ず足を運ぶ場所があった。それは、庶民のための市場やスーパーマーケットである。「市場をのぞくとその国の人や暮らしがわかるんだよ」と言いながら、その土地ならではの食べ物を試してみるのが好きだっ

of fate.

The trips to visit her children provided Mitsuko with opportunities to write her poetry. Mazatlán, in particular, became a great source of inspiration.

> *those fishermen*
> *leave everyday emotions*
> *on land.*
> *sound of the sea*
> *remains timeless.*
>
> —Akane

Mitsuko surrounded by her family including her 16 grandchildren
十六人の孫に囲まれる光子

た。また、時間があると、旅での体験や出会いを題材にして短歌や俳句を作った。

かつて光子と同じように移民として太平洋を越えた友人たちに再会するため、ブラジルやアメリカに足を伸ばしたのも、この光子70代の頃である。移住から半世紀のときが流れ、世界も、光子たち日系移民の境遇も大きく変わったことを実感する旅であった。

光子が出かけるとき、いつもハンドバックの中に忍ばせていたものがある。それは、小さな袋に入った勉の遺灰。勉の急逝から10年、20年が経ってもなお、光子の心はいつも勉とともに旅を続けていた。

by the lake
a flock of seagulls.
flying among them,
a single white butterfly,
flutters without end.
—Akane

When Mitsuko first traveled from Japan to Mexico, it took 30 days on a ship to cross the Pacific Ocean. Being able to go anywhere in the world within a day by air allowed her to indulge her ever-present curiosity about the world in her later years.

Mitsuko traveled with her children or friends to Spain, England, France, Germany, Switzerland, Vietnam, Honduras, among other countries. Wherever she went, she always made a point of going to local

Mitsuko
光子

markets and supermarkets. She would say that the local culture can be found in their markets. She was adventurous and enjoyed trying the local delicacies of every country. When there was time, Mitsuko would write a tanka or a haiku about the experiences and encounters from her trip.

Mitsuko also went to Brazil and the United States to visit the women with whom she made the journey across the ocean. Mitsuko was in her seventies. As she looked back at the changes that had taken place in the half-century since immigrating, she was reminded that both the world and the lives of immigrants, including her own, had changed dramatically.

Wherever Mitsuko went, she always kept a small pouch containing some of her husband's ashes. Even decades after his passing, Tsutomu remained in Mitsuko's heart and mind.

Mitsuko received an award from the Emperor of Japan for her contribution to the *nikkei* community
光子は日系コミュニティーの発展に貢献した功績をたたえられ日本から勲章を授与された

With the members of the Tank & Haiku Club.
In 1985, Mitsuko published *Tanka by Akane* and *Haiku by Akane*.
「句歌の集い」のメンバーと。
光子（右端）は1985年に『短歌 あかね』『句集 あかね』を出版する。

236   PART II   第二部

19. QUIET LATER YEARS

Tanka 099, 100

穏やかな晩年

Mitsuko would still visit Mazatlán into her 80s. Whenever she stayed at her daughter's home, she would help with housework or visit the factory. Everyone around Mitsuko was impressed by her vitality. However, one day Mitsuko slipped on a wet floor and fell, breaking her femur and requiring that she undergo surgery for the first time in her life.

Mitsuko was back in Mexico City, working hard on her rehabilitation, when she had the misfortune to fall again and suffer additional bone fractures. After her second surgery, she lost confidence in walking on her own and started spending most of the day inside the house.

Once known for her never-ending activity, her falls weakened her to the point that she needed to use a walker to move from room to room. Her daughter-in-law, Masako, with the help of a nurse, saw to her comfort and assisted

Wigh her six children
六人の子に囲まれて

80歳を越えてもなお、光子はマサトランを訪れていた。娘の家に泊まっては、家事を手伝ったり工場を見に行ったりして、きびきびと動く光子の姿は周りを感心させていた。ところがある日、光子は濡れた床で転んで、大腿骨を骨折してしまう。高齢のためにもろくなっていた骨はひどく砕け、光子は生まれて初めての大きな手術を経験することとなった。

メキシコシティの自宅に戻った光子は手術後毎日リハビリを行っていたが、間を置かずして再び転倒し、またもや骨折してしまう。病院での二度目の手術の後、光子は歩くことへの自信をすっかり失っていた。

この時から光子は、家の中で静かに過ごすことが多くなった。歩行補助器なしではダイニングまで歩くのも難しいほどに弱ってしまった光子を、同居していた長男の妻・正子や訪問看護師が静かに支えていた。晩年の光子の楽しみは、本を読むことだった。日本語に飢えていた数十年を取り戻そうとするかのように、自室にはいつも日本語の本が高く積み上げられていたという。読書の合間には、折に触れ詩作も楽しんだ。

her throughout the day.

As her physical body required more rest, Mitsuko's reading became voracious. As if trying to make up for decades of being too rushed with life's demands to enjoy the Japanese language, Mitsuko always kept a stack of books in her room. She also continued writing tanka between bouts of reading.

> *on the day*
> *the fragrance of sweet osmanthus*
> *fills my house,*
> *will I still be living?*
> *I wonder these days.*
> —Akane

> *seeds of*
> *the Velvet Ash bear*

金木犀の匂う屋敷となる日まで命あるやと思うこのごろ

—あかね

フレスノの種は二枚の羽根つけて未来へ向う風を待つなり

—あかね

自分の部屋で座ったまま過ごすことが多くなってからも、光子は一家の中心的存在であり続けた。この頃には何人かひ孫も誕生し、春日家は総勢四十人を数える大ファミリーとなっていた。毎週のように娘家族らが光子を訪ねてきては、世間話や思い出話に花を咲かせた。

この時期の光子は、前にもまして、感謝の言葉を口にすることが多くなっていたという。「たくさんの人々に出会って学んだことが、私の人生の宝物だ」と光子はたびたび家族に語っている。

春日光子の生涯 THE LIFE OF MITSUKO KASUGA 239

two blades.
they wait on a wind
blowing to the future.
—Akane

Even as Mitsuko spent more and more time in her room, she remained a central figure in the every-growing Kasuga family, which had surpassed forty people. Mitsuko's daughters would visit her nearly every week to share news of the family and reminisce about the past.

Perhaps it was that lack of mobility had given her more opportunity for introspection, but Mitsuko began expressing her gratitude more often. Of

Mitsuko's family supported her when she had to live with oxygen tubes due to the weakening of the lungs
肺の機能が弱くなり酸素チューブをつにるように
なった光子を家族が支えた

2002年の秋のことであった。

光子を訪ねた志保子パトリシア（光子の孫の妻）が、いつもと様子が違う光子に気づいた。同居している長男夫婦はあいにく海外に出かけていて、家には他に誰もいない。志保子パトリシアは動転する気持ちを抑えつつ救急車を呼び、光子を病院へと運んだ。

各地に散らばっていた光子の子どもたちが、呼び集められた。病室に駆けつけた親類に、光子は繰り返し感謝の言葉を伝えた。が、その呼吸は次第に弱くなっていく。

病室での静かで長い夜、娘たちは枕元で、昔光子が歌ってくれた日本の童謡を口ずさんだ。「夕焼け小焼け」、「みかんの花咲く丘」、「江戸子守唄」。光子は目を閉じたまま、じっと娘の歌声に聞き入った。

娘のエスペランサ真佐子が病室に付き添っていた夜のことだった。

光子は、ひとつ大きな呼吸をした。そして一瞬、遠く宙を見つめた。

それが光子の最期だった。

people who came to visit from Japan and people she had met through their work, she would say, "The most precious thing to me is having met them and learned from them."

During Autumn 2002, Shihoko Patricia, the wife of one of Mitsuko's grandsons, visited Mitsuko while Carlos Tsuyoshi and his wife were travelling abroad, and noticed that something was not right with her. Shihoko Patricia tried to remain calm as she called an ambulance to take Mitsuko to the hospital. Her children, scattered across the country, were called home. Family who rushed to the hospital received words of gratitude from Mitsuko.

During those last quiet, long nights, her daughters sat at Mitsuko's bedside, singing Japanese children's songs to her: "*Yuyake Koyake* (sunset glow)," "*Mikan no hanasaku oka* (hills of mandarin flowers)," "*Edo Komoriuta* (Edo lullaby)." Mitsuko closed her eyes and listened to the sounds of her children singing as her breathing weakened.

2002年10月26日、春日光子は永遠の眠りについた。移民として、母として、そして歌人として、メキシコの大地に力強い足跡を残した88年の生涯であった。

春日光子の生涯　THE LIFE OF MITSUKO KASUGA

On the night of October 26, 2002, with her daughter Esperanza Masako attending to her bedside, Mitsuko took a deep breath and briefly gazed to the sky. That was Mitsuko's last moment on this earth.

An immigrant, a mother, a teacher, a poet. In her 88 years of life, Mitsuko Kasuga left a lasting impression beyond her own family—she left behind a legacy of Japanese strength in her adoptive Mexico.

Mitsuko
光子

春日光子の生涯　THE LIFE OF MITSUKO KASUGA

The text of the Life of Mitsuko Kasuga was researched and written by Aiko Chikaba, Based on the epilogues of the books written by Mitsuko Kasuga, *Tanka by Akane*, *Haiku by Akane*, and *Suberihiyu* (Purslane) essay. Also used *Ojiichan*, written by Hermelinda Kasuga Osaka, and family albums of the Kasuga family. The tanka in this section were selected from *Milpa* newsletter (written by the Tanka & Haiku Club).

この「春日光子の生涯」の文は、『短歌 あかね』、『句集 あかね』に光子自身が記した「あとがき」のほか、長女・春日エルメリンダ美智子 (Hermelinda Michiko Kasuga Osaka) の手記『Ojiichan』、春日光子の随筆「すべりひゆ」、春日ファミリーアルバムなどをもとに、構成・執筆されました。文中に引用されている短歌は、主に「句歌の集い」の会報『みるぱ』から集めたもので、歌集『短歌 あかね』には収められていない作品が中心となっています。

BIOGRAPHY II
略歴 II

Text: Aiko Chikaba
文　近葉 愛子

Aiko Chikaba was born and raised in Osaka, Japan. She graduated from Kyoto University's faculty of letters. For nearly a decade Aiko was a director for NHK, Japan's premier TV channel. She moved to work in New York City where she also studied graphic design at NYU. In New York, she married a third-generation Japanese-Mexican, a grandson of Mitsuko Kasuga. The couple settled in San Francisco Bay Area where she currently works as a creative director.

大阪出身。京都大学文学部卒業後、テレビ・ディレクターとしてNHKの番組を多数制作する。その後、ニューヨークにてメキシコ出身の日系三世（春日光子の孫）と結婚。現在はサンフランシスコ・ベイエリアを拠点に、クリエイティブ・ディレクターとして活躍。

春日光子の生涯　THE LIFE OF MITSUKO KASUGA

Akane Immigrant Poet:
The Tanka of Mitsuko Kasuga, Japanese Immigrant in Mexico
[English Edition]

First Edition: Published on April 10, 2016
Written by Mitsuko Esperanza Kasuga, Aiko Chikaba
Translation: Naoko Shin (English Tanka) ;
               Cynthia Viveros Cano (Spanish Tanka) ;
               Carlos Ernesto Pierre-Audain Kasuga ; Aiko Chikaba
Revision: Citlali Tolia
Design: Aiko Chikaba

Printed by CreateSpace, An Amazon.com Company

Published by Texnai, Inc.
2-1 Udagawa-cho, Shibuya-ku, Tokyo, Japan, 150-0042
Tel: +81-3-3464-6927
e-mail: texnai@texnai.co.jp   http://www.texnai.co.jp/POD/

© Mitsuko Esperanza Kasuga, Aiko Chikaba

ISBN 978-4-908381-21-8

"Akane" Spanish edition available
"Akane" también disponible en español
『あかね』スペイン語版もあります（日西併記）

Akane publishing project
Proyecto de publicación Akane
あかね出版プロジェクト

We welcome your feeback!
Sus comentarios son muy bienvenidos.
ご意見・ご感想をお寄せください。

book.akane@gmail.com

www.ingramcontent.com/pod-product-compliance
Lightning Source LLC
Chambersburg PA
CBHW022355040426
42450CB00005B/194